Firesides

FIRESIDES

by
Catherine Samimi

Illustrated by

Gillian Nix

George Ronald
Oxford

George Ronald, *Publisher*
46 High Street, Kidlington, Oxford OX5 2DN

*A catalogue record for this book is available
from the British Library*

ISBN 0–85398–433–6

Cover designed by Alexander Leith
Typeset by Stonehaven Press, Knoxville, Tennessee
Printed in Great Britain by
Cromwell Press Ltd, Trowbridge, Wilts BA14 0XB

Contents

Foreword

It is the duty of every Bahá'í to convey to a world starved for spiritual regeneration the new Message of God. Bahá'u'lláh, the Author of a new Dispensation, and the Supreme Manifestation of God, revealed the following: 'God hath prescribed unto every one the duty of teaching His Cause.'[1] He exhorted us thus: 'Say: Teach ye the Cause of God, O people of Bahá, for God hath prescribed unto every one the duty of proclaiming His Message, and regardeth it as the most meritorious of all deeds.'[2] This task has been further explained by the beloved Guardian, Shoghi Effendi:

> All must participate, however humble their origin, however limited their experience, however restricted their means, however deficient their education, however pressing their cares and preoccupations, however unfavourable the environment in which they live.[3]

Teaching, therefore, is an integral element of the life of every follower of Bahá'u'lláh, a responsibility that must not be ignored. Bahá'u'lláh tells us that if a believer becomes 'kindled with the fire of His love, if he forgoeth all created things, the words he uttereth shall set on fire them that hear him'.[4] Nevertheless, in order to become effective teachers of this Cause we require training.

The field of teaching is immense and the paths for its application are innumerable. One such path iden-tified by Shoghi Effendi is the use of firesides, which he described as 'the most powerful and effective teaching medium'.[5] While the term 'fireside' is used liberally within the Bahá'í community, we may still not fully understand or apply Shoghi Effendi's vision of this important teaching tool.

This volume introduces us to the concept and application of firesides in a holistic fashion, from the personal perspective and experience of a devoted believer, Catherine Samimi. Catherine, a nurse by profession, is a member of a Local Spiritual Assembly and an assistant to two Auxiliary Board members in Alberta. Soon after she became a Bahá'í, she and her husband, Sia, pioneered to Albania for a year.

The Samimis are deeply committed to the joyous task of sharing the message of Bahá'u'lláh with as many people as possible through the medium of firesides. In this, her first book, Catherine blends a mixture of valuable references, stories and humorous anecdotes which provide practical insights into the process and art of holding firesides. This material had its genesis in a highly effective training course which Catherine offers to Bahá'í communities throughout Alberta.

I believe that this book is being made available to us at a critical stage in the growth of the Bahá'í com-munity around the world. The Universal House of

Justice indicated that 'The stage is set for universal, rapid and massive growth of the Cause of God'.[6] It explained in a letter dated September 1991:

> To be most effective, teaching needs more than proclamation. The message needs to be conveyed personally from one soul to another in a spirit of love. Shoghi Effendi talks about the 'art' of teaching. To excel in such an art requires courage, effort, constant application, the pain of uncertainty, and an enormous willingness to take risks and suffer rebuffs . . . To them must be added audacity, joy, and confident reliance on the confirmations of the Holy Spirit. Ingenuity is also required and perseverance. Although it may not be easy to meet people in order to teach them the Faith, let the friends never lose heart. There are ways if one seeks them with sufficient determination.[7]

This book, therefore, provides a timely and invaluable contribution to our efforts to apply this guidance. If its advice is systematically studied and applied with total reliance on God, it will serve as a useful vehicle to fulfil Bahá'u'lláh's admonition: 'Unloose your tongues, and proclaim unceasingly His Cause.'[8]

Riḍván Moqbel
Edmonton, Alberta
Canada

1

Why We Teach

Each One Teach One

'Each one teach one.' You've probably heard Bahá'ís use this expression. It is a common paraphrase of 'Abdu'l-Bahá's bid for each Bahá'í to share the Faith with another soul each year.[9] It is a straight forward prescription – each Bahá'í introduces the Faith to a friend, who tells another, who tells another. Soon, multitudes are embracing the Cause.

Consider this: If nine Bahá'ís who live in a town with a population of 1,000 each teach and confirm one new friend per year, and each new Bahá'í does the same, in less than seven years the entire town will be in the community of the Greatest Name. In nine more years those teaching efforts will yield a community of more than half a million Bahá'ís!

This has not yet been the pattern of growth in the Faith in North America or Europe. A handful of Bahá'ís teach tirelessly, serving as magnets for the Cause. Others watch on the sidelines, wishing they had the dedication, audacity or charisma the successful teachers demonstrate. Too few are in the middle, methodically teaching at least one new soul each year.

If each one were teaching one, there would be no need for this book. The community of Bahá'u'lláh would be expanding at old-world-order-shattering speed. The truth is, Bahá'ís need help. Myths about teaching, particularly about firesides, are hampering the progress of the Cause.

Fireside Phobia

How do *you* feel when you think about hosting a fireside? Do you anticipate it like a Bahá'í child awaiting Ayyám-i-Há? Does your stomach knot up like a piano student before a recital? Are firesides something you want to have but never seem to get around to? For some Bahá'ís, the mere thought of planning a fireside brings on nervous palpitations. Consequently, they'd prefer to avoid thinking about them altogether!

When presenting the *Successful Firesides* Workshop to Bahá'í audiences, I ask people what they think firesides are 'supposed to be'. They usually describe an evening gathering where a group of people sit in someone's living room, listen to a prepared talk, then have a discussion. Many Bahá'ís believe they don't have the ability to offer this kind of gathering in their homes. This rigid depiction of what a fireside 'should' be, and what the writings actually prescribe for us, differ. No wonder Bahá'ís don't hold as many firesides as they'd like to.

Firesides don't need fires!

For those of you experiencing fireside phobia, firesides are actually easier than you imagine. This book will help you cut through the fallacies of firesides. It will explore what is, and what is not, a fireside. It will help you develop your own style – a style of fireside that is natural to you. For Bahá'ís already experiencing the joy of holding successful firesides, this book will help launch your firesides from good to great.

Why Teach?

Before exploring techniques for having successful firesides, let's first clarify why Bahá'ís teach at all. Why should we bother with the promulgation of the Bahá'í Faith? Can't we just be happy that *we* have found Bahá'u'lláh?

To understand the importance of teaching, let's look at three points emphasized in the writings:

- our obligation to teach
- how God assists those who teach
- how teaching compares with other activities in our lives

Our Obligation

Teaching this wondrous Faith of ours is not only a source of joy, it is an *obligation*. Bahá'u'lláh actually calls it such. He wrote:

The Pen of the Most High hath decreed and imposed upon every one the obligation to teach this Cause . . . God will, no doubt, inspire whosoever detacheth himself from all else but Him, and will cause the pure waters of wisdom and utterance to gush out and flow copiously from his heart.[10]

Say: Teach ye the Cause of God, O people of Bahá, for God hath prescribed unto every one the duty of proclaiming His Message, and regardeth it as the most meritorious of all deeds.[11]

Is teaching the Faith optional? Apparently not.

Who is exempt from teaching the Cause? Here are some rationales Bahá'ís have used:

'I'm shy. I don't have many friends.'
'I'm not a good speaker.'
'I have to read more of the writings first.'
'I'm too busy. I don't have time for firesides.'
'I don't speak English (or another language) very well.'
'I'm a poor student. I hardly have any furniture.'
'I can't have guests here.'
'I'm a new Bahá'í.'
'Other people teach better than I do.'

Perhaps you've heard these and other excuses before; maybe you have even used one. The writings do not list these as exemptions from teaching the Faith but sometimes we rationalize their use. Not teaching seems easier than facing one's hurdles.

Help is on Its Way

There is no need to fear the Blessed Beauty's admonition to teach. Divine help is at hand! The following words of Bahá'u'lláh are both comforting and inspiring:

> By the righteousness of God! Whoso openeth his lips in this Day and maketh mention of the name of his Lord, the hosts of Divine inspiration shall descend upon him from the heaven of My name, the All-Knowing, the All-Wise. On him shall also descend the Concourse on high, each bearing aloft a chalice of pure light. Thus hath it been foreordained in the realm of God's Revelation, by the behest of Him Who is the All-Glorious, the Most Powerful.[12]

> Verily, We behold you from Our realm of glory, and shall aid whosoever will arise for the triumph of Our Cause with the hosts of the Concourse on high and a company of Our favoured angels.[13]

Look who is helping you teach:

- the Hosts of Divine inspiration
- the Concourse on high
- a company of God's favoured angels

What a team! Imagine the Concourse on high is at *your* fireside! Every time you open your lips to teach this Faith to another soul, the Concourse is with you. You are in great company!

I believe that most people who do not hold regular firesides do not have them because they think they are alone. They are looking at their own imagined inadequacies, doubting their abilities to forward the Cause.

The Cause of Bahá'u'lláh centres on the unfoldment of a new World Order and the spiritual transformation of the planet. This is an immense task. It would be too arrogant for us Bahá'ís to think that Bahá'u'lláh would entrust us to carry out this most important mission on our own. *Of course* He's going to help us.

How the Concourse on high descends upon us is another matter. With our human limitations, we find it hard to believe that they can be everywhere they are needed simultaneously. We imagine the Concourse helping at someone else's fireside but not at our own. 'I'm not important enough for a visit from the Concourse on high,' we think.

Omnipresence is a state of being too vast for the human mind to comprehend. The next world, however, is not restrained by time, place or matter. If Bahá'u'lláh says the Concourse on high will be there when we teach, they will be there.

Since we inhabit the physical realm, we must look after the physical details in order to hold a fireside. We invite friends, tidy our homes, prepare refreshments. Meanwhile, we must remember that the fireside is ultimately a spiritual event. The message of Bahá'u'lláh transforms hearts. As Bahá'ís, our part is to trust that Bahá'u'lláh and His 'company of favoured angels' will assist us to share His Revelation.

Deputization

> Centre your energies in the propagation of the Faith
> of God. Whoso is worthy of so high a calling, let him
> arise and promote it. Whoso is unable, it is his duty
> to appoint him who will, in his stead, proclaim this
> Revelation.
>
> *Bahá'u'lláh*[14]

Some Bahá'ís do have special circumstances that
genuinely impede their abilities to teach the Cause.
A Bahá'í whose non-Bahá'í spouse is not supportive
of the Faith might not be able to have fireside guests
in her home. A Bahá'í in very poor health might not
have the strength to travel teach, despite his yearning
to do so. Deputization enables these Bahá'ís to remain
in the stream of teaching.

There are local, national and international
deputization funds to which Bahá'ís can contribute.
A Bahá'í with financial means can donate to a
deputization fund which supports the efforts of other
Bahá'ís who will give the time and energy required
for teaching.

But deputization does not necessitate giving
money. The Oxford dictionary describes a deputy as
'a person appointed to act as substitute for another'.
Financing another Bahá'í's teaching work, or do-
nating teaching materials, is welcomed but not
mandatory.

I know a Bahá'í who suffers from depression
which renders him, at times, unable to function at his
usual level in Bahá'í community life. Not to com-

pound his depression with worries over his inability to teach, this Bahá'í has a deputy, a kind friend who is aware of his condition and gladly doubles her teaching efforts during his periods of depression. In every alternate teaching encounter she teaches in her friend's name. He contributes by praying that she meets new contacts and that these people respond to Bahá'u'lláh's message. Once a week the two Bahá'ís meet at a café and she shares her teaching stories with him. These are their joint victories. Together they have proclaimed the Greatest Name.

Teaching vs. Other Responsibilities

Every one of us has responsibilities and interests which compete for our most precious resource – our time. We go to work, prepare and eat food, chauffeur our children, serve on Bahá'í Assemblies or committees, do the laundry, mow the lawn, go to Feasts, clean the house, enjoy our hobbies, deepen, exercise, read, rest, travel – the list goes on. You have your own little merry-go-round of details called 'your life'.

How does our duty to teach the Bahá'í Faith compare with our myriad obligations and activities? Bahá'u'lláh wrote, 'Wert thou to consider this world, and realize how fleeting are the things that pertain unto it, thou wouldst choose to tread no path except the path of service to the Cause of thy Lord.'[15]

More encouragement for giving teaching the highest priority in our lives comes from the words of the Báb:

It is better to guide one soul than to possess all that is on earth, for as long as that guided soul is under the shadow of the Tree of Divine Unity, he and the one who hath guided him will both be recipients of God's tender mercy, whereas possession of earthly things will cease at the time of death.[16]

Many of our chores in life are important. After all, the writings do tell us to keep our homes and bodies clean, to become educated, to serve humanity through our work and so on. But what proportion of our time is absorbed, even wasted, on details that at the end of this life will all be forgotten?

A Bahá'í named Gordon was reconsidering the practicality of owning his large home. His family enjoyed their house and it was lovely for entertaining. Yet it required a great deal of upkeep from both him and his wife. One day while we were consulting on this subject, he asked rhetorically, 'In terms of establishing the new World Order, which is more important: Repainting my fence or teaching the Faith?' Soon after, Gordon and his wife sold their house and moved into a condominium, kids and all. The several hours per week formerly spent being slaves to their house is now dedicated to service to Bahá'u'lláh and quality family time together. They are admittedly happier.

During the *Successful Firesides* Workshop one participant put this conflict into perspective for herself and others when she mused aloud, 'Hmm. What other things do I do that the Concourse on high rushes in to help me with? Cleaning the floor? Shopping for shoes?' Well said! Which is most important in the eyes of our Lord? Sharing His message or preoccupying ourselves with material pursuits?

Notice I said most important and not just important. Many items on our personal merry-go-rounds seem important. In his book *The Ten Natural Laws of Successful Time and Life Management,* Hyrum W. Smith helps his readers differentiate between urgent and vital matters. If you intended to play with your child one evening but didn't because you were frantically typing a report for the next morning, you did what was urgent but not necessarily most important, according to your life's values. Nearly everyone would agree that their loved ones are more important than their jobs or committee service. Yet the former is often sacrificed for the latter. Why? Our families will never be urgent. They will always be there. We tell ourselves, 'I can spend time with my child tomorrow.' Smith, creator of the Franklin Daily Planner, stresses the importance of starting each day by planning our tasks in accordance with our true values. This way we can ensure that time is allotted for what we hold most dear.

For a Bahá'í, this includes obedience to God. Teaching the Faith, praying and reading the writings do not seem very urgent because no one comes by to check up on you. You won't lose your job if you don't say your obligatory prayer. You have to plan these behaviours into your life yourself. You make them urgent because you value your spiritual well-being. You might not accomplish everything on your daily 'to do' lists. The yard may not get raked today or personal letters written but if you made ample time for meditation and spent quality time with your loved ones (or did whatever else you value), then you can rest assured at the day's end that you attended to what was most important. The end result is what everyone wants – peace of mind. Teaching the Faith is a planned part of one's life, born out of an urgent desire to obey God.

Time is the greatest equalizer on earth. Some people are wealthier than others, some have better health, some are taller and others just seem to have better luck. But everyone has been dealt the same amount of time. We all have 24 hours in each day. How well we use our equal portion of time differentiates people from one another. We can spend our allotment wisely or we can waste it.

Imagine being given $1,000 every day to spend on yourself or to use to help others. The money you don't spend, however, cannot be saved for another day. It is gone forever. Would you try to put it to good use? You are given 24 whole hours every day, none of which can be carried forward. How well will you spend your daily portion?

Unworthiness

It's not unusual to feel unqualified and unworthy to carry forward Bahá'u'lláh's message. We hunger to understand it better so that we may do it justice when we share it with others. We tell ourselves, 'I need to read more Bahá'í books first, THEN I'll be ready to teach.' The truth is, we will *never* feel satisfied with our knowledge of the Faith. The more we learn, the more we know we need to learn.

The Guardian reassures us that we are all capable of advancing the Cause. A letter written on his behalf says:

> Not until all the friends come to realize that everyone is able, in his own measure, to deliver the Message, can they ever hope to reach the goal that has been set for them by a loving and wise Master. It is no use for some able and eloquent teacher to take all the responsibility for the spread of the Cause. For such a thing is not only contrary to the spirit of the Teachings, but to the explicit text of the writings of Bahá'u'lláh and 'Abdu'l-Bahá, both of whom place the obligation of teaching not in any particular class as in former ecclesiastical organizations, but on every faithful and loyal follower of the Cause. The teaching of the Word is thus made universal and compulsory. How long then shall we wait to carry out this command, the full wisdom of which only future generations will be able to appreciate? We have no special teachers in the Cause. Everyone is a potential teacher. He has only to use what God has given him and thus prove that he is faithful to his trust.[17]

If you think you need special talents to be a teacher of this Cause, look who Shoghi Effendi says is the best teacher:

A 'best teacher' and an 'exemplary believer' is ultimately neither more nor less than an ordinary Bahá'í who has consecrated himself to the work of the Faith, deepened his knowledge and understanding of its Teachings, placed his confidence in Bahá'u'lláh, and arisen to serve Him to the best of his ability.[18]

An 'ordinary Bahá'í'! That's every one of us. With dedication, deepening, faith and effort, we become the best teachers we can be.

Several excellent books have been written by devoted Bahá'ís who have shared their insights into teaching the Bahá'í Faith. Their stories inspire us to strive to do the same. Yet very little has been written specifically about firesides.

Despite the numerous ways we have to teach this Cause, the Guardian assures us that 'The most effective method of teaching is the Fireside group'.[19] Bahá'ís want to be successful in the teaching work and to see the Cause expand. Therefore, understanding and holding firesides should be an urgent priority. By improving our fireside skills, we can become confident teachers in 'the most effective method'. This book is dedicated to fireside teaching.

2

Why Firesides?

The writings make our obligation to teach the Cause quite clear. But why do we specifically need to hold *firesides*? There are plenty of other ways to teach the Faith. We talk to our colleagues at work, we invite friends to Bahá'í holy day events, we produce pamphlets, give concerts, advertise and so on. Isn't this enough?

No matter how effective all our teaching activities may be, nothing can take the place of Bahá'í hospitality offered in the warmth of one's home. That is where the strongest bonds of fellowship are established. The Guardian explains:

> The friends must realize their individual responsibility. Each must hold a Fireside in his or her home, once in 19 days, where new people are invited, and where some phase of the Faith is mentioned and discussed. If this is done with the intent of showing Bahá'í hospitality and love, then there will be results. People will become interested in 'what' you are interested in, and then be interested in studying. Individual firesides will bring the knowledge of the Faith to more people, under favourable circumstances, and thus constantly enrich its circle of

friends, and finally its members. There is no substitute for the teaching work of the individual.[20]

Notice how the Guardian uses the word 'must' twice at the beginning of this quotation. As the Guardian was ever so careful with his choice of words, this must have been a point worth stressing. He emphasizes that holding firesides in our homes, and not just teaching generally, is expected of each and every one of us.

Most Bahá'ís I meet are enthused by the prospect of sharing the Cause of Bahá'u'lláh with another person. Actually doing it is another matter. Those who are not holding firesides as frequently as they wish have concerns which include how to meet and invite new people, how to give 'a talk', how to answer their guests' questions, how to handle opposition or rejection – and the list goes on. But most surprising are the erroneous ideas Bahá'ís have about what a fireside 'should be'.

If you have ever attended a fireside in a beautifully decorated home with an eloquent and inspiring speaker and several seekers, you could easily feel intimidated if you now believe this is what *your* firesides should look like. This model of a fireside is not mandated in the writings but many Bahá'ís hold this image in their heads. Is an evening discussion group *your* impression of what a fireside 'should' be?

Keep it simple . . .

Simplifying Firesides

As mentioned above, Shoghi Effendi stated, 'Each must hold a Fireside in his or her home, once in 19 days, where new people are invited, and where some phase of the Faith is mentioned and discussed.'

What I admire most about this quotation is what it *doesn't* say. The Guardian doesn't say that in order to hold a fireside you must have a slide projector, you must have a guest speaker, you must invite as many people as possible and that a fireside must be held in the evening!

Suppose you are working in your garden on a sunny afternoon and you notice your next door neighbour is outside in his garden. The two of you stop to have a chat over the fence. It's a very hot day and you invite him in for a drink of lemonade. You're both sitting at your kitchen table, lemonades in hand, discussing when to fertilize your rose bushes this year. Your neighbour looks up at a picture of 'Abdu'l-Bahá on your wall and asks, 'Is that your grandfather?'

'No,' you answer. 'That's 'Abdu'l-Bahá, the son of Bahá'u'lláh.'

'Son of who?'

'Bahá'u'lláh. He's the Prophet/Founder of the Bahá'í Faith. His teachings are the blueprint for world peace and the unity of all humankind.'

'World peace,' he shrugs. 'I doubt that will ever happen.'

'World peace is not only possible but *inevitable*,' you suggest with a smile.

'How can you say that?' he asks.

'The Bahá'í writings refer extensively to the subject of world peace and unity,' you say.

He asks a few more questions; you answer them. He gives his viewpoint. You lovingly share yours. Gradually, the conversation drifts back to gardening and what kind of bedding plants will do well in your front yards. With your thirsts quenched, you both return to the dirt and shovels waiting for you outside.

You just held a fireside.

It wasn't planned and it wasn't long. But it was certainly a fireside. You showed hospitality to a guest in your home and discussed the Bahá'í Faith with him. *That* is a fireside.

Bahá'u'lláh gave us three daily obligatory prayers from which to choose – a long, a short and a medium length prayer. He hasn't written that He loves us more for saying a particular prayer. He just wants us to pray! The choice of obligatory prayer remains ours.

I suggest that the same principle applies to firesides. If you like to have 30 people in your living room every Thursday night and give a dazzling introduction to the Bahá'í Faith, then good for you. If you and your spouse prefer to invite another couple to your home for supper and discuss the Faith during coffee and dessert, then good for you. And if once every Bahá'í month you are able to have one friend in for afternoon lemonade, then good for you too.

Each is a fireside and each is just as worthy as the other.

The last scenario, having just one friend in for tea or lemonade, is especially useful for people whose families or roommates are not Bahá'ís. Bahá'ís in these circumstances might not feel comfortable monopolizing the living room with fireside guests for a full evening. They might, however, feel quite relaxed having afternoon tea with a friend at the kitchen table and discussing the Faith. Thus they have honoured the rights of those with whom they live.

What is a 'Fireside', Really?

Let's clear up some other misconceptions about firesides.

One day a friend rushed up to me and began excitedly talking about a great fireside he just held on the bus. He was reading a Bahá'í book when the passenger next to him asked what he was reading.

'*Paris Talks*,' my friend replied. 'It's from the Bahá'í Faith.'

'Oooh,' said the other passenger. 'I used to have a neighbour who was a Bahá'í. Nice fellow. He never said much about it, though.'

The two men then had an amicable discussion about progressive revelation. Another passenger sitting across from them joined in. Other passengers were listening, some actively, some with their heads held down and their ears cocked towards the conversation. It was one of those spontaneous encounters that leaves a Bahá'í rejoicing for the rest of the day.

But was it a fireside?

I didn't interrupt the enthusiastic story teller but I was thinking, 'Fireside? Were these people really your guests or did they pay their own bus fare? What about hospitality? Did you pull a silver tea service out of your briefcase and serve them?' I suspected not.

What my friend had was a *teaching* experience, not *fireside*. All firesides are teaching experiences but not all teaching experiences are firesides. Read that again because Bahá'ís need to be very clear about that distinction. The essential elements for a fireside are a Bahá'í host, hospitality, a guest and discussion about the Bahá'í Faith. It's that simple.

Sometimes I'm asked, 'Does it really matter?' – as if I'm being unnecessarily precise about what is a fireside and what is not. If all Bahá'ís were having frequent firesides *and* other teaching encounters, it probably wouldn't matter what these events were called. If, however, the doors of hospitality in Bahá'í homes remain closed while other encounters are being called firesides, then *it matters*. Bahá'ís still need to follow the Guardian's exhortation to hold regular firesides in their homes.

All our teaching work is important but nothing is more effective than the intimacy of the fireside. The Guardian said:

> The most effective method of teaching is the Fireside group, where new people can be shown Bahá'í hospitality, and ask all questions which bother

them. They can feel there the true Bahá'í spirit – and
it is the spirit that quickeneth.[21]

In a letter written on his behalf, Shoghi Effendi also
said:

> The primary duty laid upon all Bahá'ís by Bahá'u-
> 'lláh, Himself, is to teach the Cause of God. It is their
> greatest privilege and bounty. They should seek
> out receptive souls, mingle with all classes, races
> and denominations, and find amongst them those
> who are receptive to the spirit of God, and then
> with wisdom and love lead them to take the great
> step of acknowledging the Manifestation of God
> for this Day. Not only must the friends be encour-
> aged to teach in their Ḥaẓíratu'l-Quds, through
> public meetings and study classes, they must also
> be encouraged to teach in their homes at what the
> Americans have called 'firesides'. This personal
> loving contact does more to confirm new believers
> than any other one thing.[22]

Teaching at Seekers' Homes

The importance of extending Bahá'í hospitality and
love to our guests in our homes is clear. But what if
our contacts invite us to *their* homes? Is this our fireside? Technically, no. We are visiting them.

Invariably this happens. You have guests to your
home for fireside dinners or coffee and eventually
they present the reciprocal invitation. They do want
to meet with you again but they are offering to be the
hosts. No, it doesn't 'count' as *your* fireside because

you are not extending Bahá'í hospitality in your home. This doesn't matter. Fortunately, teaching the Cause of God is not about keeping score. There are no trophies for having several monthly firesides in one's home. If your contacts want to host you sometimes, let them. You still have 18 other days during which to host them or other guests for a fireside in your home.

Several times at larger firesides in our home an inspired guest has asked of all present, 'Can we all do this again next week at my place?' If our non-Bahá'í guests want to hold firesides in their homes, albeit with our contacts, my husband and I support them! We find writings on the topics that interest them and make a presentation if they wish. Usually, the gatherings are casual group discussions, fueled by seekers' questions and no prepared talk is required. The new hosts usually invite other friends of theirs too. Then the circle of seekers expands. Teaching the Faith themselves is the best way for seekers to become consecrated in the Faith.

Such a fireside group will meet back at our home again and continue to alternate between seekers' homes and ours. Seekers meet each other at firesides and become friends. A close circle of rotating firesides develops. One by one the seekers enrol in the Faith, having been the witnesses and supporters of each others' critical journeys in spiritual transformation.

Must Firesides be Monthly?

One workshop participant asked, 'Do we really have to hold a fireside once in every 19 days? Isn't that being really picky? Can't we just use that as a loose guideline to follow?'

I'll share with you the wise answer offered by another workshop participant. He said, 'I believe that holding firesides at least once in a Bahá'í month is for our own spiritual benefit. The regularity of it is part of our spiritual discipline. It's not acceptable to say 365 obligatory prayers on the first day of the year and think we are excused for the rest of the year. So, no, I don't think we can "bank" firesides and skip them in other months.'

I like his answer.

The Origin of the 'Fireside'

Do you wonder where the term 'fireside' comes from? It began with May Maxwell, the mother of Rúḥíyyih Khánum and eminent teacher of the Bahá'í Faith. Mrs Maxwell wrote to Shoghi Effendi describing how she would introduce the Faith to guests while sitting at the fireside in her Montreal home. In the early 1900s the fireplace was the source of heat for a home and the fireside was the most hospitable place to seat guests.

The Guardian wrote back to her, encouraging her to continue holding these 'fireside talks'. In subsequent letters the Guardian refers to hospitably teaching the Faith in one's home as a 'fireside'. Through these letters, the word 'fireside' became a part of Bahá'í text. Now the term 'fireside' is used to describe this form of teaching, no matter what home heating method is used, be it a fireplace, gas furnace or solar panels!

It is not by accident that you are reading a book about firesides. By picking up this book you have demonstrated that you are enamoured with this Cause and feel compelled to share it with others. A major component of that is holding firesides. Understanding one's obligation to teach this Faith and recognizing the assistance God provides are the first steps. Now let's explore some practical techniques that will kindle your way to fireside success!

3

Getting Started

Prayer

After acknowledging our obligation to teach the Cause of Bahá'u'lláh, then what? If you're frozen fearfully in your tracks, or perhaps are gleefully leaping ahead, pause for a moment. Get centred. Begin your fireside planning with prayer.

What would one be praying for at this stage? Some possibilities include:

> courage
> detachment
> divine assistance
> spiritual qualities
> eloquence
> victory
> teaching contacts
> staying focused, committed to the Covenant
> guidance
> finding teaching materials

The list is endless. Praying for teaching contacts not only means praying that we attract seekers but that we are actually praying *for* them. We pray that our contacts receive both the spiritual guidance they need and assistance with their personal problems.

A young Bahá'í couple shared the following story:

Shortly after we were married, we made a commitment together to hold regular firesides. We decided to say the [following] teaching prayer [attributed to] 'Abdu'l-Bahá at least twice a day:

O Lord! Open Thou the door, provide the means, prepare the way, make safe the path, that we may be guided to those souls whose hearts are prepared for Thy Cause and that they may be guided to us. Verily, Thou art the Merciful, the Most Bountiful, the All-Powerful.[23]

In addition to praying, we both very consciously looked for opportunities to invite people to firesides. Within two weeks we had eight firesides scheduled for the next month! That taught us never to under-estimate the power of prayer!

Daily Reading

Bahá'u'lláh encourages us to memorize His writings. Paraphrasing the writings never does them justice, nor does it carry the potency of the Divine Word. Bahá'u'lláh wrote:

The sanctified souls should ponder and meditate in their hearts regarding the methods of teaching. From the texts of the wondrous, heavenly Scriptures they should memorize phrases and passages bearing on various instances, so that in the course

of their speech they may recite divine verses whenever the occasion demandeth it, inasmuch as these
holy verses are the most potent elixir, the greatest
and mightiest talisman. So potent is their influence
that the hearer will have no cause for vacillation. I
swear by My life! This Revelation is endowed with
such a power that it will act as the lodestone for all
nations and kindreds of the earth. Should one
pause to meditate attentively he would recognize
that no place is there, nor can there be, for anyone
to flee to.[24]

Have you thought about the impact that daily
reading of the writings has upon our firesides? Not
only does daily reading deepen our knowledge of
the Faith, strengthen us in the Covenant and nourish
our souls, it also helps us quote the writings un-
adulterated and we become better vehicles for the
presentation of the Bahá'í Faith.

You may have had the experience of discussing the
Faith with friends, Bahá'ís or not, when suddenly an
appropriate quotation rolls off your lips, unabridged.
Your Bahá'í friends look at you quite impressed,
wondering if you've memorized *Gleanings from the
Writings of Bahá'u'lláh*. You're impressed too! 'What
a coincidence we are discussing this right now,' you
say. 'That was my morning reading today!' No coincidence at all. It happens frequently to Bahá'ís. The
more we read, the more we remember and the more
occasions we have to use what we have read.

By loyally reading the writings at least every morning and evening and making the effort to memorize

some of them, we give ourselves greater ability to quote and recall. We never know when this will prove useful. In turn, being able to recite the holy verses increases our level of confidence at our firesides too.

There is a very wise saying: 'What you behold you become.' What do *you* behold? The Bahá'í writings? Or would you rather behold television soap operas? If you watch them regularly, you could be teaching yourself that gossip is acceptable and relationships disposable. Beholding pornography convinces some people that impersonal sex is okay. Some people attracted to martial arts movies admit to fantasizing about being heroes and solving problems with violence. Heavy metal and rap music with violent lyrics may channel otherwise useful youthful energy into attitudes and behaviours that are not beneficial to humankind.

On the other hand, listening to a baroque symphony can inspire tranquillity. Admiring a beautiful sunset may foster reverence. Reading Bahá'u'lláh's writings every day moves us towards what He desires we become. Beholding the holy word every day can help us embrace the Covenant with the loyalty of martyrs.

Here is a revealing exercise. Ask yourself what you behold (on TV, in books, in your mind or anywhere) and sincerely ask yourself how they have influenced what you have become. Are there any adjustments you'd like to make?

Myth-Busting

In order to create a good foundation on which to build your firesides, it helps to first clear away the rubble left behind from any erroneous beliefs. It's much easier to move ahead when you're not tripping over things that don't belong. Let's sweep away some more fireside myths.

Myth: 'I should have a guest speaker'

Some people's firesides have made history because they have attracted large numbers of people and have reputations for having dynamic guest speakers. That's only one type of fireside. In fact, its among the least common. But because of their fame, that style has crept into many Bahá'ís' visions of what a 'good' fireside looks like.

Once in a while my husband and I like to invite another Bahá'í to present a topic at our firesides, when we feel our guests would benefit from hearing from someone other than us for a change. But usually we just have a casual chat with our guests, unaided.

Bahá'ís sometimes call us to be guest speakers at their firesides. Before accepting, we like to find out why we've really been invited. If the hosts want to give some variety to their regular guests or feel we'll have better social chemistry with certain guests, we'll accept. But if the hosts say that they don't know how to give a talk, we try to help the hosts become the type of fireside presenters they naturally are. Usually they're planning a type of fireside that isn't suited to either themselves or their guests. When we accept invitations to such firesides we keep our own 'presentation' relaxed, just to show the hosts that their own firesides don't need to be structured ordeals. They shouldn't have performance anxiety in their own living room.

You don't need a conversational pinch-hitter when you're having a casual discussion with a friend and you don't need one for your firesides either.

Myth: 'I need to prepare a talk'

When you have a friend in for coffee, do you worry and research what you'll talk about? Of course not! Someone starts with 'How are you? What have you been doing lately?' and the conversation takes care of itself. Hours can pass and you don't refer to notes for what to say next. Your fireside can, and should, flow that comfortably.

There is a time and place for prepared fireside presentations. In fact, advertising the fireside topic on fliers and in newspapers can be a way of attracting new people. I emphasize again, though, this is often a poor way to start. If you've just taken up jogging, signing up for a marathon in your first week would put unnecessary stress on your mind and body. When starting firesides, don't plan something that is bigger than feels right for you. You can invite one or two friends in and chat the way you've been doing all your life. Just as you would discuss your job, your family and other interests in your life, details of your Bahá'í life should naturally come up in conversation. The Bahá'í Faith is an integral part of who you are and it is only natural for it to be mentioned when catching up during a visit with friends.

Myth: 'A good fireside has lots of guests.'

Not all firesides are alike. Thank goodness, because not all seekers are alike either! You are a unique individual, needed on planet Earth to teach the Bahá'í Faith to the people who are attracted to *you*. So what is your personal style of fireside? Let's find out.

There are different settings in which Bahá'ís can teach the Faith in their homes. There is the evening discussion group. (I hope the myth of this being the ideal fireside has now been put to rest!) You can hold a small dinner gathering for a couple of friends or just invite them over for coffee and dessert in the evening. You can invite a friend over for afternoon tea or have a few friends in to play cards. You might meet parents of your children's friends. Youth can hold firesides by having a slumber party. You may have a neighbour who doesn't seem comfortable coming into your house but will gladly accept an invitation to a barbecue in your back yard. Many people have co-workers who show no interest in coming to an evening discussion on religion. Yet if those same people are presented with the statement, 'My husband/wife and I would love to have you and your husband/wife over for brunch this Sunday.

Would you like to come?' they will often accept and be flattered that you asked.

Are you wondering, 'Isn't it deceitful to invite people to your home without telling them you want to introduce the Bahá'í Faith to them?' If they arrive and find other people there who are prepared for a discussion on the Faith, it is. They'll feel like they've been ambushed into a sales presentation. There is, however, nothing dishonest about having a friend in for a visit. As part of getting to know each other better it is only natural that your being a Bahá'í will come up in conversation.

The Guardian's statement quoted above asserts that at a fireside 'some phase of the faith is mentioned and discussed'. More than once I have had the experience of mentioning the Faith with no discussion taking place. For example, a friend asked to see my photos of our year pioneering in Albania. 'Why did you go there?' she asked. 'We were volunteering for the Bahá'í Faith,' I replied. Despite my inserting tidbits about the Faith throughout our conversation, she only asked about the living conditions in Albania and then talked about her own travels. The Faith was mentioned but not discussed. This seldom happens, as most people have the social grace to show a little interest in what is meaningful to another person. This meeting did not become a fireside. Not every attempt at a fireside yields fruit, yet it remains noble to try. I never feel guilty having a friend in for tea, with the hope that the Bahá'í Faith will be one of the many things we talk about.

If it weren't so sad, I would find it funny when I hear Bahá'ís say, 'I'm holding regular firesides but nobody comes!' And its often said in a tone of voice that suggests, '*I'm* doing *my* part but the guests aren't doing *theirs!*' If your firesides are repeatedly unattended, **re-evaluate your style of fireside**. It's not working.

In these cases, what usually happens is this: The hosts plan an evening discussion group but they invite brunch or barbecue type guests. The invitees aren't interested in what they perceive has been planned by the hosts. It's a mismatch. If you learn only one thing from this book, I hope it is this: Planning big evening meetings is seldom the best way to start holding firesides. You could be headed for a great deal of disappointment. Before you have successful evening group firesides, you usually need to host a number of individual meetings first. You need to develop an assortment of contacts, who, if showing some interest in the Faith, will later come back to a larger fireside. The disappointment of having no one come to your evening firesides after all your efforts in planning and inviting people is an avoidable heartbreak.

For many guests, an invitation to a presentation and discussion, especially if they feel cautious about religion, has about as much appeal as going to the public library to watch a documentary video. Unless it's a subject they are eagerly interested in, there's no strong commitment to attend. People think to themselves, 'Maybe I'll go, maybe I won't. I'll decide at the

Some invitations have about as much appeal as going to the library to watch a documentary

last minute and go only if there's nothing better to do.' When being invited to someone's home for a discussion, people often feel uncomfortable saying 'no' directly to the host. It's easier to say 'I'll try to make it' and just not show up.

Now compare that to a dinner invitation. Suppose your family invites another family to your home for supper. You agree on a date and time and everyone says they are looking forward to being together. Would your friends simply not show up, knowing that you are cooking for them and anticipating their visit? Probably not! If an emergency arose and they truly could not attend, most people would call to inform their hosts and apologize for postponing the evening.

You *should* feel confident that your firesides will have guests present. Both parties should be looking forward to being in each other's company. I recently met a Bahá'í friend at a grocery store and mentioned that the snacks I was buying were for a fireside we were having that night.

'How many people are coming?' she asked, then quickly added, 'Well, I guess one never really knows, do they!'

'Six,' I replied.

'Oh, really?' She looked puzzled, wondering how I could possibly be so sure.

We had been having small firesides with several friends, one or two guests at a time. Once their interest in the Faith was evident and they had come to a couple of firesides each, we asked if they would like to meet other people like themselves who were investigating the Bahá'í Faith. The term 'fireside' was explained to those who had not yet heard it. They all showed interest. They were attracted to the idea of meeting other people who might have the same questions or challenges they had and learning from questions asked by others. After their first fireside together, they all agreed to continue studying the Faith together every one to two weeks. That's how we were certain there would be six fireside guests that evening. They had all committed to come.

Several times my husband, Sia, and I have introduced individual fireside guests to each other and they have chosen to continue studying the Faith together. The guests develop a bond and support each other's growth. In one fireside group, a common concern was fear of their parents' reactions if they became Bahá'ís. The first person who enrolled in the Faith became a role model for the others. 'What did your mother say?' was the reaction of the others. (And these were all 30–something adults!) 'It really wasn't as hard as I imagined it would be,' she responded, and continued to share her story with them. As the months went by, the other members of the group enrolled one by one, helping each other over various hurdles. Ultimately, the fireside became a deepening group because they were now all Bahá'ís! (They nicknamed their meetings 'deepensides'). My husband and I continued to study with them until they became integrated into the Bahá'í community and eventually began holding firesides of their own.

In this group, there was a great deal of personal confidential information shared. It would not have been appropriate to add a new member to the group once they started meeting together. When my husband and I met new contacts, we held separate firesides for them. Those who chose to continue investigating the Bahá'í Faith were later introduced to other seekers and a new group formed. An error in judgement I see repeated by Bahá'ís is to invite more people to a fireside just because the host is already expecting one or more guests. This is often done without considering if that particular mix of guests is truly in the best interests of all the guests involved. Depending on the compatibility of individuals and their level of knowledge about the Bahá'í Faith, adding newcomers is not always appropriate.

A Bahá'í, Mira, relayed the following story:

Whenever I hold group firesides with people I hardly know, seldom are these firesides comfortable for either the guests or myself. We all usually feel awkward. Some such firesides even feel like disasters! In one month, four different friends had given me names of strangers to invite to firesides at our home. The names were forwarded to me by Bahá'ís who lived in other towns and had contacts in our city and by local Bahá'ís who wanted their contacts to meet us. Feeling 'behind' with our fireside dinners, my husband and I invited those four strangers to one fireside, along with four of our own acquaintances whom we felt overdue inviting to a fireside. We made the eight phone calls. If all eight individuals had been able to come, the evening may have turned out all right. But the least desirable combination occurred. Only two guests were available. We had an elderly gentleman whose knowledge of the Faith was quite deep. He came with specific questions about some obscure writings from Bahá'u'lláh. The only other guest was a new immigrant who barely spoke English and whose Bahá'í knowledge was limited to having heard of a few of the principles of the Faith.

That was a very long, uncomfortable evening for everyone, as you might guess! We essentially had two simultaneous firesides happening in the same room. My husband and the male guest delved into *The Seven Valleys and the Four Valleys*, while I explained to the young woman that the principles she admired were actually part of a religion whose Prophet was Bahá'u'lláh. They were both very nice people; they also had little in common and weren't benefiting from each other's questions. We should have had them over separately and given them each our full attention. If a large group of people had attended that fireside, both of these guests would have somehow blended in. Everyone would have benefited without these two particular guests feeling they had to make conversation with each other.

Another Bahá'í, Farshid, described holding a fireside to which he had invited six friends of similar ages and interests, though they had not met each other before. All six invitees came and still the gathering was awkward for the host.

None of the guests had met each other before and none of them had ever been to a fireside. I thought that it would be a better fireside if I had lots of guests there. I imagined everyone having a good discussion together. But that's not how it went at all. I gave a talk about something, I don't even remember what it was about. Then I tried to involve people in a discussion but it didn't happen. If I asked a question generally, nobody answered. If I asked one person what he thought, he'd give a really short answer. I felt I was having the whole conversation by myself. It was awful. So I just served the pie and we talked about other things.

Farshid concluded that the guests at this fireside were shy in front of each other and weren't sure how to behave at a fireside. If one or two of them had been to a fireside discussion before and had become more involved that night, it might have set the stage for others to join in. In hindsight Farshid wishes he'd invited them individually or with guests he could count on to contribute to the conversation.

Other Bahá'ís have had experiences of gathering strangers together and having the firesides be magical! The chemistry amongst the guests has been magnetic and the guests have become close friends with each other. A host can never predict the outcome of mixing strangers at a fireside. Again I wish to emphasize that this is a pitfall for so many Bahá'ís – thinking that the group fireside is the way a fireside is 'supposed' to be held. As a responsible host, always consider the mix of your guests.

Some Bahá'ís have a reputation for having large weekly firesides. Their home is well-known by seekers as a place where they can drop in for spiritual rejuvenation, glad that there will be a room full of other seekers who are also curious about the Bahá'í Faith. Perhaps you wish your home was such a place. It may well be some day! But don't expect your firesides to begin this way. They evolve. Begin by teaching your current friends. They are your friends because they are already attracted to you. Now *that's* a comfortable and reliable way to have a conversation. Then, if you want your small firesides to grow into larger ones, there can be a natural progression. Seekers may even start to bring their friends to your firesides. Your little firesides can blossom into larger ones through their own momentum.

Finding Your Style

If you're like me, when you're reading a book and the author asks you to pause to do a written exercise, you say to yourself, 'Good exercise. I'll keep reading and come back to it later.' And never do. I recently did the unthinkable. I was reading a book on time management and I actually stopped and did an exercise! It greatly impacted my life. And wasn't that why I was reading the book in the first place? I wanted to grow beyond my present condition. If I was really going to let the author help me, I needed to follow his advice.

Now I'm asking you to venture into the same realm. Take a risk and do the exercise. If I promise this will be the only exercise in the book, can you promise to take a time-out and do it? You'll enjoy the rest of the book more if you do. Here we go:

Take a sheet or several sheets of paper and draw lines dividing the page(s) into quadrants. Label each square with a type of fireside that you might be able to give, now or in the future. Choices include:

lunch
supper, small and casual
formal dinner party
brunch
afternoon tea
evening dessert (one or two guests)
large evening discussion group, casual
large group with guest speaker
barbecue
slide or video presentation
kids having a slumber party
doing crafts together
playing games
musicians' jam session

You'll think of more. If you believe you give your best firesides in your hot tub, then hold them in your hot tub!

An innovative way to introduce several people to the Faith at once is to hold an 'open house' on the occasion of a Bahá'í holy day. Anna and Hamed do this every Naw-Rúz. They shared the following story:

We invite all our neighbours, co-workers and other acquaintances to drop by any time on Naw-Rúz. Last year it was on a weekend and we had a steady flow of visitors all day! It was wonderful! We had a buffet table full with special food and we even decorated the living room with ribbons and flowers. We had Bahá'í books and pictures visible, which started a few conversations. Lots of people were curious why we celebrate new year on March 21st and not January 1st. Naw-Rúz is a good teaching opportunity for us. We invited a few Bahá'í friends too, to help with serving and visiting with our guests. Every guest who came learned that this was the Bahá'í New Year; most of them left having learned a little more about the Faith too. Last year we missed going to our community's holy day celebration because we still had several guests in our home! It was our greatest fireside ever!

Whom Will I Invite?

Next, list names of people you could invite in each category. Remember, this is only a list of *potential* fireside guests. Making the list is not an obligation to call anyone. It's just a list that helps you consider who your possible teaching contacts are. Give your mind permission to allow the names of people you know to come to your consciousness and write their names down somewhere on the pages. Many names will appear in more than one column, since some people could be invited to more than one kind of fireside.

As a variation:

Draw columns/quadrants on paper and list people in categories by which you know them, such as work, neighbours, relatives, school, sports team mates, volunteer groups, etc. One useful category is 'old friends' – people with whom you already have a rapport but haven't seen for a while. Fireside or dinner invitations are great ways to rekindle old friendships.

Include service people on your lists. You might never invite your barber home for supper but you might feel okay mentioning as he cuts your hair, 'Henry, I'm a Bahá'í. Tomorrow evening I'm having some friends in for a discussion on (you fill in the blank), and I'd really like it if you could join us. Besides, my wife makes a great cheese cake!' Henry might not be interested. But what if he says, 'I didn't know you're a Bahá'í! I've been reading about it lately! I'm so glad you told me!' How will you ever know whether your barber is a seeker if you don't give him the chance to tell you?

And if Henry only comes for the cheesecake, that's just fine. He'll still hear something about the Faith. I know a Bahá'í who admits he used to go to firesides because he liked free cookies. He wasn't particularly interested in the Faith back then. But something must have rubbed off on him. He's now an Auxiliary Board member and a very audacious teacher.

Teaching relatives

Teaching Relatives

Relatives. Sometimes these are the last people Bahá'ís want to teach. We know what their religious beliefs are and we don't want to open ourselves up to their judgement or rejection. Instead of trying to teach family members for their own sakes, hoping they will recognize Bahá'u'lláh, another approach is often more effective and generally more comfortable for all of you. Consider telling them, 'I've become a Bahá'í and this is very important to me. I want to tell you about it but not to try to convert you. I just want to share with you something that has greatly impacted my life and is an important part of who I am now.' Because of their pre-existing love for you, relatives are often willing to listen if the Bahá'í Faith is introduced in this manner. They tend to show interest and ask questions because they are concerned *for you*, not necessarily because they wish to investigate this religion for themselves.

One July, Martin had relatives staying in his home for a week. On the ninth, the anniversary of the martyrdom of the Báb, he cooked a special supper. After the meal, while everyone was still seated at the table, he asked if he could share a special story with them. He explained that today was a holy day for Bahá'ís and asked their permission to share why this day was so important to him. Martin then recounted the story of the martyrdom of the Báb. There were children present and Martin dramatized the story to hold their interest. There was suspense, imaginary smoke and gunfire. They could almost smell the gunpowder. The children were engaged as if they were listening to a good bedtime story, while the adults listened courteously. Without preaching, Martin was able to tell his loved ones something about this Faith that is so dear to him. He held a fireside.

Overcoming Fear

When doing this exercise and making your lists, it is natural to think of a name of a potential guest and suddenly feel, 'Eeek! I don't have the courage to invite *him*!' I'd like to offer you two techniques that can help prevent that block.

First is a trick for feeling fearless. We will borrow a technique from therapists who counsel chronic worriers. There are people who are so preoccupied with worrying that it impairs their daily functioning. The therapist tells the client that he may worry intensely for a set time period each day, say one hour. The client sets aside one uninterrupted hour to focus all his attention on the item(s) he worries about. After the hour is over, the client must do something else. He is not to set his thoughts on his worries until the appointed hour comes the following day. Simply knowing that he will have an entire hour tomorrow scheduled for worrying has proved to be effective in enabling clients to be more productive during the day. The client is eventually weaned to 45 minutes, then half an hour and so on.

You will use this model in reverse. For 20 minutes you agree *not* to worry. As the name or face of each potential fireside guest appears in your mind, do not judge the person's reaction to your fireside or the invitation. You just joyfully write his name down on your page. Later, you can look at your list and worry if you like! For now though, you will let all the names flow.

Another helpful technique is to imagine each person accepting your invitation. Picture each one saying, 'Yes, I'd love to come. Thank you for inviting me!'

Now you're ready to make your list. Put on some nice background music if you like, sit in your favourite spot. Be in a private place, as when you meditate. Start with a prayer, then let the names come to you. Go ahead. We'll meet back here after you're done.

* * *

How was it? Most Bahá'ís say they find this exercise useful. Their memories are jogged and they think of potential fireside guests who have never occurred to them before. We're surrounded by teaching opportunities!

One workshop participant didn't want to do this exercise. Her professional background was in sales and this reminded her of making lists of people to try to sell her product to. Those lists of her friends' names were for making sales, not for true friendly visits. She didn't want to become a sneaky peddlar of the Bahá'í Faith. Selling a commercial product is not spiritually based, at least not in many of the businesses I've seen! It's about closing yet another deal. If calling up friends and acquaintances to invite them to firesides feels insincere, then don't do it. Only invite people whom you genuinely want to have visit in your home. Friends who have an expressed interest in the Faith are easy to invite to firesides. You can even use the term 'fireside' with them. If you don't currently have these kinds of contacts, then a list of possible invitees is helpful. It gets you started and gives you a reference point when you need it. The Bahá'í saleswoman who said she didn't want to make a fireside contact list also knew she wouldn't need one. Her household has a constant flow of visitors. Discussing the Faith with at least one of them in 19 days would be natural.

Another Bahá'í in the same workshop was having her kitchen remodelled. 'Surely I'm exempt from having a fireside this month!' she said. 'My home is a mess! I can't entertain with construction materials lying everywhere.'

'Will there be *anyone* in your home this month to whom you could mention the Faith?' I asked her.

'Only relatives and construction workers,' she said. Then she smiled. She saw possibilities.

Unless you are a hermit living in a cave without any contact with another soul, you probably have people in your home at some time or another each month or at least have the opportunity to have people in. The key is to recognize the teaching opportunities that already lie within your daily life.

Myth: 'Firesides should be held every week.'

In addition to what type of firesides to hold and who to invite, another question Bahá'ís ask themselves is how frequently to hold firesides. The Guardian simply tells us once in 19 days. For many Bahá'ís, no set day is best. They like to stay flexible to accommodate the days that are best for their guests. For others, committing to weekly firesides is their way of disciplining themselves to have firesides.

One Bahá'í couple admits that they need the structure of having weekly firesides. 'We know that Friday nights are our fireside nights. If we left it unscheduled, we might not even make it once in 19 days. It's our way of keeping teaching a priority in our lives.' What kind of fireside schedule is best for you?

Someday you will look at names on the list you have just written and you will feel differently about them. People who you once thought you wouldn't have the courage to call are now easy to invite. Maybe you're becoming a better teacher of the Cause, maybe your friendships with certain people have grown closer and so on.

* * *

Keep your list. You will need it later, maybe many months later. The challenge is not to discard it during a moment of fear or doubt. You will feel fearless again. Someday you will be wondering who you can invite to a fireside and you will be glad to have your reference list.

But I don't know anyone to talk to about the Faith!

4

Preparing for the Fireside

You have prepared yourself both mentally and spiritually to hold firesides. Now it's time to take action.

The Invitations

An invitation to a fireside can be as casual and spontaneous as phoning a friend and saying, 'Want to drop in for supper tonight? It won't be elaborate but we'd sure like to see you!'

One workshop participant said that she isn't a fancy cook and isn't shy about serving left-overs to friends. 'If I thought I had to cook a gourmet meal for guests, I'd really cut down on my firesides!' she laughed.

This was a real revelation to her neighbour. The Bahá'í had invited her next-door neighbour and family in for supper. She served chili and bread. Her guests loved it. The neighbour, a gourmet cook, confessed that she had always felt that cooking for company had to be an elaborate production. She seldom entertained, fearing she wouldn't meet her own expectations. Seeing chili served came as a relief to her and helped her reduce her expectations of herself.

Look at your list of guests and fireside settings and ask yourself where you'd like to begin. Start with the easy ones – friends you know well or people who have already expressed their interest in the Bahá'í Faith to you. If you start planning firesides with people who frequently break appointments, this can be discouraging. Realistically, cancellations cannot always be avoided. It is therefore helpful to plan more than one fireside per month. If one fireside is cancelled, it is not so disappointing if you have another to look forward to. If both firesides take place, all the better!

If you're just starting to have firesides, planning the first few requires the most courage. Believe me, once you've had a few firesides with interested guests in dynamic discussions, you will be so excited you won't be able to wait for the next time! Successful firesides are addictive. Holding firesides honestly gets easier once you walk yourself through the initial trepidation of getting started.

Some Bahá'ís print attractive invitation cards, advertising different fireside topics every month, and distribute them in their neighbourhoods. This method may take time to develop a small regular crowd. For some persistent Bahá'ís, however, this technique has proved fruitful.

Work out a plan for your fireside

The Preparation

You've invited people to your home for a fireside and they've accepted. Now what do you do? That depends on how much lead time you have. For most of us, the thought of having guests over invokes one immediate thought: 'I need to clean the house!'

A Bahá'í couple who have weekly firesides told me, 'Having a fireside every Friday is great! We know we're going to fully clean our house once a week. Our place has never been so clean!'

Most of us don't have the luxury of hired help to clean the house and we always feel somewhat behind with housework. You clean it, then a few days later it looks like it needs it again. 'Abdu'l-Bahá was very conscientious about household cleanliness. So I hope He forgives me when I admit to sometimes doing the ten-minute-pre-guest-house-cleaning-routine: dishes are quickly hidden in the dishwasher, bathroom taps are shined (this gives the illusion of having cleaned the entire bathroom) and the living room is spot-dusted. There. I'm done. Ready for the guests I just invited. This isn't how we live, of course. We do wash our dishes, our vacuum gets taken out for a walk around the house once in a while and the bathroom gets a regular good going over. But, like the gourmet cook, if I thought I had to have a spotless house before ever letting someone in, that would greatly reduce my firesides. And nothing so material is going to prevent me from having a fireside. I'm confessing to the ten-minute house cleaning facade in case you thought you were the only one doing it!

On with the rest of your preparation. You might bake or buy some goodies. I make a big batch of cookie dough and freeze it in smaller portions. If we have guests at short notice, home-baked cookies are ready in no time and provide an inviting aroma too. Fresh baked cookies also freeze well and thaw in minutes. 'I haven't got anything to serve' shouldn't be the thought preventing a Bahá'í from spontaneously bringing home a guest. Just serving a beverage or store-bought snacks is perfectly acceptable hospitality, accompanied by your friendly warmth.

For the planned-in-advance fireside, you can prepare a little better. Pay attention to the ambiance of your home. Imagine how the guests will feel the moment they walk in. You can create a magnetic environment that will attract seekers to your Bahá'í home and make them feel instantly welcome and at ease. Fresh flowers or a scented candle add to the aroma and beauty of a room. Music playing quietly in the background helps people feel relaxed. A Greatest Name symbol hanging on your wall not only shows that this is a Bahá'í home, it also confers blessings.

If you've decided to give a talk, you'll prepare one. (Keep your notes. You can use them again with other guests.) If you want to show a video, you'll find/borrow that video.

In some parts of the world, people wanting to become Bahá'ís need to fill in declaration or registration cards. In the countries where this is the case, I ask participants in the *Successful Firesides* Workshop, 'Do you have declaration cards in your home?' Surprisingly, the majority say no.

'If you had a fireside guest who said "I want to become a Bahá'í", what would you do?' I ask them.

Most of them stare upwards, half smiling, as if they have just had a new insight. Having someone declare his belief in Bahá'u'lláh in their home is not something they have anticipated happening.

We hold firesides to help other people discover Bahá'u'lláh's healing message for humanity. We should expect results! Someday someone will be in your home asking how she can become a Bahá'í. Be ready for her.

Prayer

Your house is clean and refreshments are ready. Your home is welcoming. You've got 20 minutes before your guests will arrive. What will you do?

I strongly urge you not to fuss around until the last minute. Say some prayers instead. Create a peaceful, prayerful space for yourself and centre yourself. You are about to share Bahá'u'lláh's revelation with someone. Stop and ask for His help.

'Abdu'l-Bahá said:

I say unto you that anyone who will rise up in the Cause of God at this time shall be filled with the spirit of God, and that He will send His hosts from heaven to help you, and that nothing shall be impossible to you if you have faith. And now I give you a commandment which shall be for a covenant between you and Me – that ye have faith; that your faith be steadfast as a rock that no storms can move, that nothing can disturb, and that it endure through all things even to the end; even should ye hear that your Lord has been crucified, be not shaken in your faith; for I am with you always, whether living or dead, I am with you to the end. As ye have faith so shall your powers and blessings be. This is the balance – this is the balance – this is the balance.[25]

Your powers and blessings in teaching the Cause are equated with your faith. And when you have faith, nothing shall be impossible to you. Pausing to read the writings and to say prayers before a fireside is invaluable.

Fireside Host Anxiety, or 'What Not to Do!'

I'd like to share two stories about hurried hosts who were nervous before their impending firesides. Neither had taken time to pray and centre themselves, as you will see.

Two sisters I know had been having weekly firesides for a few months. They would invite whomever they could think of to drop by on Thursday evenings for a fireside. Sometimes they'd have one guest but usually none. Having read Chapter 3, you already know why these firesides were poorly attended. The invitation wasn't personal enough for guests to commit themselves to attending.

Don't leave your preparations until the last minute

Concerned that the hosts were getting discouraged, I asked if one of our contacts could attend their fireside. A friend of mine, Karen, was regularly attending various firesides at our home. I thought she would benefit from meeting Bahá'ís other than ourselves. The sisters – we'll call them Holly and Rita – invited Karen to a fireside. The morning after the fireside Karen phoned me to relay the following comedy of errors.

When Karen arrived at the house, Rita answered the door wide-eyed and out of breath.

'Uh-oh,' thought Karen. 'She's not ready and is panicking about it.' As Karen entered the foyer, she was greeted by the odour of burnt cake wafting through the air. Her hostess led her into the sitting room, kicking books and newspapers under a chair as she passed by. Rita gestured to Karen to sit on the couch.

As Karen started to sit, Rita burst out with, 'Wait! Maybe you'd rather sit here.' Rita gestured towards a chair. 'Or maybe you'd be more comfortable over here,' pointing to yet another chair. 'Or maybe you'd be most comfortable on the couch,' she sighed.

Like a VCR stuck on 'pause', Karen stood partially bent, unsure whether to sit where she was or move to a chair. 'I'm fine here,' she said, and finished lowering herself onto the couch.

Holly came out of the kitchen, wiping black crumbs from her hands onto her skirt. Her task must have been to try to salvage some dessert.

Introductions were performed. Everyone was seated. There was silence – awkward silence. Rita and

Holly suddenly jumped up together, excused them-selves and dashed into the kitchen.

Rita eventually returned with a tray bearing tea and water. There was a jingling noise coming from somewhere. As Rita lowered the tray for Karen to help herself to beverages, Karen saw the water glasses bouncing against each other and the teacups tap-dancing in their saucers. Poor, nervous Rita. She was a one-woman earthquake trying to serve tea.

Holly returned with cake for everyone. She apolo-gized that the top had been cut off. Karen, their polite guest, said she liked it that way.

After they ate their cake, Rita broke the silence with, 'Prayers! Shall we begin with prayers? Do you like Bahá'í prayers? What do you want to do? Should we pray?' She looked right at Karen.

'Please do whatever you usually do. I'll be fine with that,' Karen smiled. She admitted to me that she was really thinking, 'I just want to get out of here!' They all felt uncomfortable. Karen graciously hung in there. The evening improved because it couldn't have got any worse. The hosts gradually relaxed and eventually a meaningful discussion about the Faith took place.

I'm glad the fireside ended well. Today, all three women are close Bahá'í friends. The mishaps were preventable, though. No Bahá'í wants a guest to think 'I just want to get out of here' during his fireside. Look at your home and your firesides through the eyes of your guests and ask yourself what kind of ambiance exists there.

The other story is my own experience of being the awkward hostess.

Suzanne, a young woman who had come to a couple of our firesides, asked if she could bring her fiancé. We said we'd be delighted to meet him and invited them both to join us for supper two weeks later.

The appointed day finally came. I was nervous about meeting a new person and forgot to make time for prayer. It was five minutes to six o'clock. I mentally went through my checklist: 'The casserole will come out in 20 minutes, the pie will bake while we eat, mellow music is on the stereo, the dining table is set, I tidied up the –' Then our apartment door buzzer rang. 'Honey, they're here!' I yelled down the hall to my husband, who was cleaning the bathroom. 'Come on up!' I said into the intercom and buzzed in our guests.

'Okay! They're coming up the elevator now. They'll be here in a minute.' I was talking to myself out loud. I usually love entertaining and having firesides, yet on this occasion I was all nerves. 'I'm going to say, "Hello, Raymond. My name is Catherine. I'm pleased to meet you. Please come in."' Yes, that's what I'm going to say!' Rehearsing introducing myself. I was sinking fast.

Finally, there was the knock on the door. With my husband at my side, I swung the door open wide. There stood Suzanne and Raymond, smiling, flowers in hand. As they crossed the threshold, I began energetically shaking the young man's hand with both of mine. Not letting go, I then blurted out, 'Hello! I'm Raymond!' Despite all my practice, I got my own name wrong.

Everyone stood still, staring at me. My first choice was to suddenly wake up from what was obviously just a horrible dream. I waited. Nothing happened. O God, I must have really said that! (When one is already nervous, embarrassment cuts even deeper.) Maybe no one noticed my mistake.

'Suzanne!' I said. 'How lovely to see you!' and I flung my arms around her. Over her shoulder I could see my dumbfounded husband still staring at me. Okay – they noticed.

Whether we're tripping physically or verbally, it is usually best to just admit we're falling and get it over with. The more we try to recover and hope no one has noticed, the more attention we draw to ourselves.

Fortunately for my ego, the evening proceeded without anyone mentioning my embarrassing slip-up. That is, until our guests went home. They left our apartment and my husband closed the door behind them. He slowly turned around and said, 'Hello, I'm *Raymond*? How could you have said that?' He then fell to the floor, laughing. He was laughing so hard, no sound was coming out. After a full minute of unsuccessfully trying to defend myself, I finally joined him. We both lay in our entrance way, giggling and jiggling, too weak to get up.

Notice that both of these stories involve having fireside guests whom the hosts had not met before. Perhaps there's a lesson in that. All the more reason to start by inviting people with whom you already feel comfortable.

The writings talk about extending 'Bahá'í hospitality'. This means creating a friendly environment for

your guests to walk into. You only have a few seconds to make a first impression. Be warm, be inviting.
Above all, be relaxed. If you're stressed, your guests
will know it. Make time for prayer and read from the
writings before a scheduled fireside. It is worth it!

Food: In Good Taste

When entertaining several guests, some fireside hosts
have a tendency to prepare too great a variety of
desserts. Their hospitality is well-intentioned but too
much food can backfire at a fireside. Have you noticed what people talk about when they are circling
a table of food? They talk about food!

> 'This looks delicious! Have you tried one of
>   these?'
> 'Mmm. Chocolate! My favourite!'
> 'I wonder how she made this.'
> 'I'd love to get the recipe for this one.' And so
>   on.

People who train others to give home-based sales
parties (for kitchenware, make-up, clothing, etc.)
suggest serving only one or two dessert items, so as
not to lose the audience's attention. You can apply
the same reasoning to your firesides. If people have
to leave the sitting area to serve themselves refreshments, it could be difficult to return the conversation
to the subject of the Faith once they are re-seated.
Instead, pass a couple of plates of goodies around the
room where everyone is gathered. This enables your
guests to sample your creations but does not interrupt
the discussion. Including a fruit option or a light

savoury is appreciated by guests who may be diabetic or dieting.

Your home and refreshments are now ready. You have focused yourself with prayer and meditation. Now, let's move into the heat of the actual fireside.

We're only here for the food!

Prepare for your fireside

5

Frequently Asked Questions

Fundamental Verities

Many Bahá'ís are hesitant to hold firesides because they fear guests will ask questions they cannot answer. They fear embarrassment or not knowing something they think they are 'supposed' to know. If Bahá'ís had to 'know it all' before they could speak to others, there wouldn't be any firesides at all!

When we've accepted that we'll never know all there is to know about the Bahá'í Faith, we *can* prepare ourselves with a few basics. Understanding the fundamental verities of the Faith is a sensible beginning. Verities are truths. The fundamental verities of the Bahá'í Faith are its basic truths. It is not possible to discuss all the verities of the Faith here. By reviewing the verities discussed in other Bahá'í sources, you can feel confident that you are solid in the basics.

If a fireside guest asks you how many Hands of the Cause there were and you don't know, just say, 'I don't know.' There's no shame in saying you need to look something up. But if that guest asks if Bahá'ís believe the Universal House of Justice really is infallible, be prepared to say an unhesitating 'Yes!' not 'I think so'. The infallibility of the Central Figures and the Universal House of Justice is a cornerstone of our Faith.

> *Guest*: 'Who can interpret the writings of Bahá'u'lláh?'

> *Bahá'í*: ''Abdu'l-Bahá and Shoghi Effendi.'

> *Guest*: 'Not the Universal House of Justice?'

> *Bahá'í*: 'No, but the Universal House of Justice can *legislate* on matters based on the interpretations of Bahá'u'lláh's writings by 'Abdu'l-Bahá and Shoghi Effendi.'

> *Guest*: 'Can't individuals interpret?'

> *Bahá'í*: 'They can interpret the writings for themselves in their own attempt to understand Bahá'u'lláh's teachings but they cannot present their own interpretations to others as fact or try to persuade them to agree.'

In this example the Bahá'í was clear as to what the writings say regarding interpretation of the Bahá'í scriptures. Her knowledge enabled her to provide a clear and unwavering answer to her guest.

Our loyalty to the Covenant must be steadfast. As you are a Bahá'í, even if you are still wrestling with some concepts taught by the Bahá'í Faith, the Covenant requires that you unquestioningly state the verities as they exist in the writings. Continuing to study and grow in one's understanding of the verities is integral to being a Bahá'í.

What exactly are the fundamental verities of the Bahá'í Faith? There is no list that says 'these are the essential things one must absolutely know about the Faith'. In fact, in a letter of 12 November 1996 the Universal House of Justice wrote, 'As you can see, there is no absolute list of fundamental verities and the friends should not make an issue of this matter by attempting to codify these verities.' Shoghi Effendi outlined most of the verities in his letter known as *The Dispensation of Bahá'u'lláh* and encouraged all of us to study and understand them. By continuing to read the writings daily and by taking advantage of the deepening classes made available to us, we will gradually strengthen our footing in this mighty Cause.

Influence

Influence is an interesting thing. In the workshop, when I ask participants, 'Is it proper to try to influence your fireside guests?' those who respond quickly say, 'No, of course not', as if influence implies pushing one's belief upon others.

The Oxford dictionary describes influence as:

1. The power to produce an effect, *the influence of the moon on the tides*. 2. The ability to affect someone's character or beliefs or actions.

When we tell a child 'Set a good example. Eat with your fork, not your fingers. Your little sister is watch-

ing you', we want him to influence the character and
behaviour of his younger sister. This is creating a
positive influence.

As an international community of Bahá'ís, we
respect men and women as equals, we desire a world
commonwealth of nations, we strive to lessen the gap
between wealth and poverty.

Do we want our prayers, words and actions to
exert a positive influence upon the world? Absolutely!

Wanting to influence someone, or even the whole
world, with the Bahá'í Faith is not a selfish thing.
Remember, we mortals did not invent the new World
Order. It is the Word of God, that *divine* influence,
that will transform the hearts of humankind. By
sharing it with others, we facilitate the mysterious
powers of this revelation to influence human souls.
Bahá'u'lláh wrote:

> Every word that proceedeth out of the mouth of
> God is endowed with such potency as can instil new
> life into every human frame, if ye be of them that
> comprehend this truth.[26]

'Abdu'l-Bahá says the following about influence:

> The teacher should not consider himself as learned
> and others ignorant. Such a thought breedeth pride,
> and pride is not conducive to influence. The teacher
> should not see in himself any superiority; he should
> speak with the utmost kindliness, lowliness and
> humility, for such speech exerteth influence and
> educateth the souls.[27]

So, go ahead. Be a conduit for the influential words of Bahá'u'lláh! (A selection of Bahá'í writings using the word 'influence' can be found in the Appendix.)

Frequently Asked Questions

Some questions seem to surface regularly at firesides. Whether you love them, fear them or are tired of answering the same old questions, they keep right on appearing. 'Why are there no women on the Universal House of Justice?' 'Why are the writings written in such old English?' 'What do Bahá'ís believe about homosexuality?' 'Can't you drink alcohol just once in a while?' and so on.

In this chapter we will explore some questions frequently asked by fireside guests. Then we will look at some pertinent writings on these subjects. Fireside hosts should be grounded in what the writings actually say before presenting answers to seekers' questions as facts. Remember, saying 'I don't know' or 'Let's look it up' is always allowed.

We will then observe, through dialogue, effective responses some Bahá'ís have given to these common questions. These are transcripts of actual discussions held in firesides. They are not presented here as the only or best possible answers; these were actual conversations appropriate to the people involved. These dialogues allow you to eavesdrop on how some real-life Bahá'ís have handled some real-life firesides.

Avoid floundering and later regretting not saying what you *could* have said. By giving some forethought to these questions, and reading the writings pertaining to them, you can prepare yourself for some common, and sometimes difficult, questions.

'What is the Bahá'í Faith?'

You get in an elevator. There is one other person in it. He looks at your T-shirt, which reads 'One Planet, One People – Please. Bahá'í Faith.' He asks you, 'What is the Bahá'í Faith?' You have a few seconds in which to answer him. Enough time for one sentence. One *really good* sentence. What do you say?

Several Bahá'ís describe being in situations just like this one and going blank. The elevator doors open again and the stranger leaves before the Bahá'í finds his voice. The Bahá'í Faith is much too vast to sum up into one sentence! Yet without an answer a teaching opportunity is lost. The question came unexpectedly and the Bahá'í wasn't prepared.

Get prepared! What is your one-sentence explanation of the Bahá'í Faith? What is your one minute 'sound-bite'? If you have five minutes at a bus stop with a seeker, what are the essential points you want to leave with him?

I did a role-play exercise with a group of new Bahá'í youths. They were 12- to 15-year-olds who had been Bahá'ís for between two months and two years. In the exercise one youth played the role of a Bahá'í and another was a friend he met on the street. The question 'What is the Bahá'í Faith?' was to occur

Some people choose the most awkward moment to ask about the Faith in their conversation. A typical dialogue went like this:

> 'Hi! How are you! I haven't seen you for a long time!'
> 'I'm fine. How are you?'
> 'Fine. Where are you going?'
> 'I'm going to a Bahá'í youth meeting.'
> 'What is Bahá'í?'
> 'We believe in equality of men and women, we don't drink alcohol, and – um – we have Feasts – and – um – uh –'

Each pair of youths had a turn at the exercise. Most of their role-plays went just like the one above. They stumbled. They mentioned a couple of principles. They all mentioned alcohol for some reason. Then they ran out of things to say.

These youths needed to learn what to highlight to an inquiring friend. To help them focus, I asked them to name out loud what they felt were the essential elements of the Bahá'í Faith, while I wrote their suggestions on a large sheet of paper we had taped on the wall. They said:

- Unity
- Love
- Going to deepening classes
- World peace! We don't want war.
- Equality of men and women
- You're supposed to consult.
- We should say daily obligatory prayers.

- Going to 19 Day Feast
- Bahá'ís don't drink alcohol.
- Fasting
- Bahá'u'lláh
- 'Abdu'l-Bahá
- Local Spiritual Assembly
- Unity of religions. Everybody should get along together.
- You should help the poor people and people who are starving.
- Reading the writings
- Giving to the Fund
- Backbiting is bad

I asked them, 'Is the Bahá'í Faith a religion or just a nice club?'

'It's a religion!' they said.

'Is it part of another religion or is it independent?'

'It's independent!' They were amazing themselves with how much they knew.

They decided to add 'independent world religion' to their list.

I then asked them as a group to pick the three most important items from their list and form a one-sentence answer to the question 'What is the Bahá'í Faith?' This would take some time. They were about to practise their own consultation skills.

They eventually came up with this:

The Bahá'í Faith is an independent world religion that promotes world peace and the unity of all mankind.

They were so proud. They did it! They were able to state what they believed the Bahá'í Faith stood for in one compact sentence. The process of formulating this sentence also clarified what the Bahá'í Faith meant to the youths themselves.

Next I asked them what their second sentence would be. This was more difficult. Everything on their list was important to them. Nonetheless, they were able to compose the following:

The Prophet of the Bahá'í Faith is Bahá'u'lláh, who gave us laws and principles to live by.

Amazing! They eventually recognized that in their initial role-playing and on their master list hanging on the wall, they had highlighted *individual* laws and principles. One law does not represent the whole Faith and therefore need not be mentioned in the first breath explaining the Bahá'í Faith to another person. Saying that there *are* laws and principles for humanity to live by makes a better introduction.

How do *you* respond to the question 'What is the Bahá'í Faith?' Your answer could be similar to the one created by the youths. You might have different answers for different occasions. In some cases you might feel that a mysterious answer is called for, like 'The Bahá'í Faith is the solution humanity has been waiting for' or 'It's the most beautiful thing I've ever encountered!' if you think these responses will intrigue a particular questioner. But do have a response! The question 'What is the Bahá'í Faith?' can come when you least expect it. Are you ready for it?

'Why are there no women on the Universal House of Justice?'

We have decreed that a third part of all fines shall go to the Seat of Justice, and We admonish its men to observe pure justice, that they may expend what is thus accumulated for such purposes as have been enjoined upon them by Him Who is the All-Knowing, the All-Wise. O ye Men of Justice! Be ye, in the realm of God, shepherds unto His sheep and guard them from the ravening wolves that have appeared in disguise, even as ye would guard your own sons. Thus exhorteth you the Counsellor, the Faithful.

Bahá'u'lláh[28]

It has been elucidated in the writings of 'Abdu'l-Bahá and Shoghi Effendi that, while the membership of the Universal House of Justice is confined to men, both women and men are eligible for election to Secondary and Local Houses of Justice (currently designated as National and Local Spiritual Assemblies).

The Universal House of Justice[29]

The House of Justice, however, according to the explicit text of the Law of God, is confined to men; this for a wisdom of the Lord God's, which will ere long be made manifest as clearly as the sun at high noon.

'Abdu'l-Bahá[30]

As regards the membership of the International House of Justice, 'Abdu'l-Bahá states in a Tablet that it is confined to men, and that the wisdom of it will be revealed as manifest as the sun in the future. In any case the believers should know that, as 'Abdu'l-Bahá Himself has explicitly stated that sexes are equal except in some cases, the exclusion of women from the International House of Justice, should not be surprising. From the fact that there is no equality of functions between the sexes one should not, however, infer that either sex is inherently superior or inferior to the other, or that they are unequal in their rights.

Shoghi Effendi[31]

The principle of Faith is to accept anything the Manifestation of God says, once you have accepted Him as being the Manifestation. That is really the crux of the whole matter. It is a question of confidence.

From a letter written on behalf of Shoghi Effendi[32]

'Why are there no women on the Universal House of Justice?' Have you heard this one before? No doubt! Eventually all seekers want this explained to them. Do you wish you knew the answer? The fact remains, we don't. This is often not good enough for our fireside guests. They want an answer and they expect you to give one. If you don't know the definitive answer, they'll press you for your best speculation. Herein lies a great danger for Bahá'ís.

I have heard Bahá'ís offer their personal opinions to non-Bahá'ís as to why women do not serve on the House of Justice. Each time I want to shake my head and bury my face in my hands. The Central Figures of the Faith did not reveal to us why women do not serve on the House of Justice. Nor did they tease us with possibilities. The members of the House do not offer personal speculations, no matter how frequently they are urged to do so by curious Bahá'ís!

The answer is clear. Someday humankind will have the answer to this question and it will 'be made manifest as clearly as the sun at high noon'. Subject closed. Once a Bahá'í offers his own speculation, even if he prefaces it with 'this is simply my own opinion', it is too late. You cannot turn back the conversation once you've voiced your own speculations on this subject. The non-Bahá'í is then free to find holes in your theories, speculate upon your speculations and even create a few of his own. For example:

Guest: 'Why can't women be on the Universal House of Justice?'

Bahá'í: 'Maybe its because women have babies and raising children well is an important full-time commitment.'

Guest: 'That means that infertile and post-menopausal women should be allowed to serve on the House of Justice, right?'

Bahá'í: 'Well, no, they can't.

Guest: 'Why not, if they're not having babies?'

Bahá'í: 'Maybe that's not the reason then. As I said, it was just my own idea.'

Guest: 'So, what else could it be?'

> *Bahá'í*: 'I don't know. Maybe its because there could be a war and women are exempted from fighting in war.'

> *Guest*: 'Lots of women these days serve in the military and they're doing great. Besides, top military officials aren't out on the front lines of battle. Women could serve on the House of Justice and be the generals!'

By now the Bahá'í is wondering how he ever got caught in this conversation. He did it himself when he dared to speculate in the company of his non-Bahá'í guest. I don't condemn Bahá'ís for being a little curious about this subject themselves. I do, however, object to Bahá'ís voicing their speculations in front of fireside guests. There is nothing to gain from it and plenty to lose.

DIALOGUE

Here is a conversation that took place between a Bahá'í and a fireside guest on the same topic. It's not the only way to answer this question but it avoids many of the potential dangers of speculating on an answer.

> *Guest*: 'Is it true that women can't be on the Universal House of Justice?'

> *Bahá'í*: 'Yes, that's right. The Universal House of Justice members are men.'

Guest: 'But how can that be? Everything else I've read about this Faith says that men and women are equal.'

Bahá'í: 'They are equal. They're also different.'

Guest: 'But if women can't be on the highest governing body of a religion, that's not equality. That's patriarchy.'

Bahá'í: 'Equality of people does not mean sameness. Equality refers to one's intrinsic rights and value as a spiritual being, not to one's function. Women can give birth. This doesn't mean men are inferior beings because they can't do that. That's an example of having a different function.'

Guest: 'So what is the different function that makes men eligible for the Universal House of Justice and not women?'

Bahá'í: 'I don't know. None of us do yet. We have been reassured by 'Abdu'l-Bahá, though, that eventually the wisdom of it will 'be made manifest as clearly as the sun at high noon'.

Guest: 'When will that be?'

Bahá'í: 'I don't know.'

Guest: 'Who does know?'

Bahá'í: 'Only God.'

Guest: 'But *I* want to know! This House of Justice thing really bothers me!'

Bahá'í: 'I also wonder about it sometimes and so do other Bahá'ís. But I also trust God's timing in all things. If God has a reason for revealing this knowledge later and not now, I must have faith in His supreme wisdom.'

Guest: 'I think the Bahá'ís should put some women on the Universal House of Justice. Your public image would be better. It would prove you really believe in equality of the sexes. Everything else in your Faith supports equality and then you go and have this House of Justice problem. It doesn't look good.'

Bahá'í: 'The laws of the Bahá'í Faith were given to us by Bahá'u'lláh in His book, the Kitáb-i-Aqdas. We can't change them. Bahá'ís cannot pick the parts they like and change the rest. It's a package deal. It's okay to not understand some things as Bahá'ís, such as why there are no women on the Universal House of Justice, but the authority and wisdom of the Word of God remain unquestioned.'

Guest: 'Okay, I can appreciate that. But I'm still curious.'

Bahá'í: 'Do people know where the sun is at noon or do they look up, complain about the darkness and ask others if anyone has seen the sun?'

Guest: 'Okay, the noon sun is pretty obvious. So you're saying that the reason why the Universal House of Justice is men only will eventually be that obvious?'

Bahá'í: 'Yes. The writings assure us it will be that clear.'

Guest: 'That's good enough for you? Don't you want to know *now*?'

Bahá'í: 'I have moments of curiosity but I don't dwell on it. I shouldn't want anything for myself that God doesn't want for me. I simply have to be patient.'

Guest: 'When do you think God will make this clear as the sun?'

Bahá'í: 'I don't know. Maybe not in my lifetime. All I can do is be patient and have faith. The fact that the Universal House of Justice members are men is not an equality issue for Bahá'ís. It's a matter of faith. We trust Bahá'u'lláh.'

You might not be able to satisfy all a seeker's questions on this subject. Your best balm for a friend puzzled by this feature of our Faith is to display your own peace with this issue. Your faith in God and willingness to wait for the noon-day sun are your answer.

'Why are the Bahá'í writings in archaic English?'

> We have noticed a tendency in a number of countries to attempt to translate Bahá'í literature into the current, easy, everyday language of the country. This, however, should not be an overriding consideration. Many of the Tablets of Bahá'u'lláh and 'Abdu'l-Bahá are in exalted and highly poetic language in the original Persian and Arabic and you will see, for example, that when translating Bahá'u-'lláh's Writings into English the beloved Guardian did not use present-day colloquial English but evolved a highly poetic and beautiful style, using numbers of archaic expressions reminiscent of the translations of the Bible.
>
> *The Universal House of Justice*[33]

> It is, of course, permissible to translate Bahá'í Writings into other languages and dialects of languages. It is also possible to simplify or paraphrase the Bahá'í Writings in order to facilitate their translation into languages and dialects having small vocabularies. However, it is not permissible to publish simplifications and paraphrases of Bahá'í Writings as Bahá'í Scripture.
>
> *Written on behalf of the Universal House of Justice*[34]

DIALOGUE

Here is a conversation that took place between a fireside guest and a Bahá'í trying to answer this question.

Guest: 'I find the Bahá'í writings hard to read. Why are they written in such an old form of English? Nobody talks that way anymore.'

Bahá'í: 'The Guardian of the Bahá'í Faith, Shoghi Effendi, made some of the first translations of the holy writings into English. He was educated at Oxford University with the purpose of perfecting his English so he could best translate the writings. He chose an archaic form of English because it best captured the richness and beauty of the Persian and Arabic from which he was translating. Persian and Arabic are old, poetic languages. Preserving that richness during translation required a brilliant and meticulous translator. That was Shoghi Effendi. Translation continues today and the translators follow the standard originally set by the Guardian. Colloquial English is ever changing; a word is popular today and gone tomorrow. The Bahá'í era, which is for a thousand or more years, requires a form of English that will endure beyond linguistic fads.'

Guest: 'But why use male-oriented words? Why "O Son of Being" when "O Child of Being" works just as well? It would help a lot of women feel more included in this religion. How can I say "because this son hath arisen to render Thee service" when I'm a woman? Can I not say "because this daughter" or "because this child"?

And why is God referred to as "He"? Can I substitute "She" or "Creator"?'

Bahá'í: 'You've hit upon a subject that is dear to many people in the West, where great efforts are being made to use "politically correct" language whenever possible. Some religious groups are even reprinting their holy books with gender neutral terms. If Bahá'ís were to change things in their writings, where would it stop? It might innocently begin with changing a few "Hes" to "Shes" and "Fathers" to "Creators" but what if the next person wants to put a few women on the Universal House of Justice or change the "year of patience" to the "month of patience"?

'God is an Unknowable Essence, beyond human comprehension, human language and the human tendency to see things in terms of gender. Although the use of "masculine" words does occur in the writings, Bahá'ís totally trust the wisdom of the Messengers of God, even if they cannot yet understand it. We must strive to understand the writings; we don't change them to make ourselves feel more comfortable.

'You might find it interesting that there are other parts of the world where the style of the Bahá'í writings is not an issue. Those people instead have struggles with other aspects of the Bahá'í Faith that are easy for *you*, such as a husband actually consulting with his wife. This doesn't answer your question but I hope it shows your struggle in a broader context.'

Guest: 'Yeah, okay, but I still find it hard to read the writings when they're full of old words like "thee" and "thou". It really slows down my reading.'

Bahá'í: 'Do you speak another language?'

Guest: 'I speak some French. Why?'

Bahá'í: 'Try reading Bahá'í prayers in French. You won't have the same problem. There are no "thees" and "thous". "Tu" is used, which is the common word, like "you". That's true when reading the writings in most other languages too. The problem isn't the Bahá'í writings; it's the limits of the English language, wonderful as it is. People who have learned Arabic and Persian are able to read the writings in their original, beautiful forms. I hear it touches them in a way the translations do not.'

Guest: 'Yes, English has its pitfalls but it still bugs me that the Bahá'í writings use masculine pronouns. I'm really wrestling with this!'

Bahá'í: 'So wrestle. It's okay to be bugged by something. If you leave this topic alone for a while you may find that when you come back to it, it looks different to you than it did before. It might annoy you less. Someday the language of the Bahá'í Faith might not bother you at all

– but you'll have found something new to wrestle with! That's growth!'

'Don't Bahá'ís drink alcohol?'

Regarding the use of liquor: According to the text of the Book of Aqdas, both light and strong drinks are prohibited. The reason for this prohibition is that alcohol leadeth the mind astray and causeth the weakening of the body. If alcohol were beneficial, it would have been brought into the world by the divine creation and not by the effort of man. Whatever is beneficial for man existeth in creation. Now it hath been proved and is established medically and scientifically that liquor is harmful.

As to the meaning of that which is written in the Tablets: 'I have chosen for thee whatsoever is in the heaven and the earth', this signifieth those things which are in accordance with the divine purpose and not the things which are harmful. For instance, one of the existing things is poison. Can we say that poison must be used as it hath been created by God? Nevertheless, intoxicating liquor, if prescribed by a physician for the patient and if its use is absolutely necessary, then it is permissible.

In brief, I hope that thou mayest become inebriated with the wine of the love of God, find eternal bliss and receive inexhaustible joy and happiness. All wine hath depression as an after-effect, except the wine of the Love of God.

'Abdu'l-Bahá[35]

Such a chaste and holy life, with its implications of modesty, purity, temperance, decency, and clean-mindedness, involves no less than the exercise of moderation in all that pertains to dress, language, amusements, and all artistic and literary avocations. It demands daily vigilance in the control of one's carnal desires and corrupt inclinations. It calls for the abandonment of a frivolous conduct, with its excessive attachment to trivial and often misdirected pleasures. It requires total abstinence from all alcoholic drinks, from opium, and from similar habit-forming drugs. It condemns the prostitution of art and of literature, the practices of nudism and of companionate marriage, infidelity in marital relationships, and all manner of promiscuity, of easy familiarity, and of sexual vices. It can tolerate no compromise with the theories, the standards, the habits, and the excesses of a decadent age. Nay rather it seeks to demonstrate, through the dynamic force of its example, the pernicious character of such theories, the falsity of such standards, the hollowness of such claims, the perversity of such habits, and the sacrilegious character of such excesses.

Shoghi Effendi[36]

At one fireside the inevitable subject of alcohol came up. Present were a married couple in their 40s, another man in his 40s and a student in his early 20s. All four had met each other at previous firesides and were enjoying exploring the Faith together. All of them drank alcohol. None was an alcoholic, though each admittedly appreciated a few glasses of a favourite liquor now and then.

'But why shouldn't you be able to drink a nice glass of wine with dinner if you want to?' came the not-so-new question. 'I mean, if a person doesn't abuse alcohol and drinks moderately and responsibly, is there really any harm?'

I paused for a moment, formulating my response. Pauses are wonderful. They allow time for a wiser person than oneself to answer instead. This time the wiser soul was the same woman who asked the question. She continued:

'Well, I suppose it's hard to regulate something like that. What would society say? "Person A can keep drinking because he only has one beer on the weekends but person B, who gets drunk twice a week, is no longer permitted alcohol"? If Bahá'u'lláh's teachings are for everyone, then they have to be the same for all of us. After all, a law is a law. If *some* of us could drink, which would then keep the liquor stores in business, alcohol would remain temptingly available to people with drinking problems. For someone like me, who considers myself a harmless social drinker, giving up alcohol would be my contribution to building a better society for everyone. That makes sense.' She then laughed. 'Gosh, I would miss my liqueurs!'

During that four-hour fireside, the three older guests spoke a lot. The young student hardly said a word. Each time we asked if he wanted to offer any thoughts, he said, 'No, I'm just listening.' Knowing that partying with his friends was a pleasurable part of his life, I observed that this particular fireside was challenging him. He wasn't ready to stop boozing with his buddies. His three fireside comrades appeared to be inches away from declaring their faith in Bahá'u'lláh and on this day they were unknowingly testing him with the thorny issue of alcohol.

That night I felt reasonably confident that the three 40-somethings would show up at our next fireside with their declaration cards signed. As for the student, well, he might back off for a while. When will I learn to stop judging when others will become Bahá'ís? I was wrong on all four counts. The student became a Bahá'í the next day.

'That fireside was great for me!' he said. 'Everything I needed to hear about alcohol was covered! That was my last barrier. Now I want to be a Bahá'í!' He followed his heart and it led him straight home – home to Bahá'u'lláh. The three 40–somethings needed several more weeks before they enrolled in the Faith, as their rational minds wrestled with a few more obstacles.

We had another fireside with those same four guests soon after the 'alcohol' fireside. It was in the first week of January. The 40–somethings, though not yet Bahá'ís, all announced they had quit drinking alcohol on New Year's day. The married couple shared an amusing story about how they had told their best social drinking pals they would no longer be getting tipsy with them.

It was customary for the two couples to share wine or liqueurs during their monthly visits together. New Year's Eve was no exception.

'We're going to enjoy drinking with you this evening as we ring in the New Year,' they told their friends, 'but after tonight we will not be drinking anymore. We've been investigating the Bahá'í Faith and, as we've told you before, drinking alcohol is not permitted for Bahá'ís. Tonight we will pack up all our booze and send it home in a box with you.'

'Sure you will!' their guests laughed. This must be a joke.

The two couples drank, laughed and talked for hours. By two a.m. the guests were preparing to go home.

'We'll get the booze for you now,' said the hosts. They placed all their bottles of liquor in a box and handed it over to their friends at the front door.

'You're kidding, right?' said the bewildered guests.

'No kidding. It's all yours now.'

Concluding that their hosts were not behaving sensibly under the influence of alcohol, the guests gave them another chance. With an unopened six-pack of the male host's favourite beer under his arm, the male guest whispered to his friend, 'Come over tomorrow afternoon and we'll open this together.' He winked as he backed out of the door.

The guests left with their arms full of liquid treasure, assuming they were only holding it in trust for their temporarily insane friends. In the days that followed, they were assured their friends' 'insanity' was indeed here to stay.

'WHAT WILL PEOPLE THINK?'

'What will others think?' is a big concern for many almost-Bahá'ís who have a history of drinking in certain situations. There are fears of not being understood or supported by relatives, going to business lunches with the boss where having a drink is the unwritten rule, or wondering if one can go out with drinking friends and have a soft drink without being chastised.

Most Bahá'ís I talk to who have been in these situations say their fears were worse than reality. The anticipation of informing others that they no longer drink caused more agony than the actual moment of disclosure. Not everyone will understand why obeying this law is important to the new Bahá'í but generally people respect each other's decisions, especially when they are morally or religiously based. If a lot of ridicule is directed towards the new Bahá'í simply because he no longer drinks alcohol, he may want to reevaluate who he calls his friends.

BEING TESTED

Remember the student who readily declared his faith in Bahá'u'lláh after the 'alcohol' fireside? Six months later he went to the home of another Bahá'í to consult on a personal matter.

'Sometimes I find it really tough, not drinking at all,' he blushed. He hadn't touched alcohol since becoming a Bahá'í and was now struggling.

'Did you think you'd never have another craving?' asked his friend.

'I was hoping so,' replied the student.

'Becoming a Bahá'í is a beginning, it's not an end,' his friend told him. 'There are lots of challenges ahead. If Bahá'ís appear to have their lives together on the outside it doesn't mean they're not struggling inside. We all are. That's why we're here. To grow spiritually. One person might feel tested by chastity, another by fasting, another by his own subtle racial prejudices. For you and me the challenge is alcohol.'

The student was surprised. '*You* find not drinking a test?'

'Sure I do.'

'How often do you think about it?'

'More days than not.'

'Have you ever had a drink since becoming a Bahá'í?'

'Not once. And I'm not going to.'

'How can you be so sure?'

'I'm not. I just want to be sure. So that's what I tell myself.'

'One day at a time, right?' smiled the student.

'One day at a time. Do you want to say some prayers together?'

They prayed. Knowing that he was not alone boosted the student's strength to accept his struggle and confront it with dignity.

Growing up in a Bahá'í household where Bahá'í laws are as familiar as one's name and alcohol is not present in the home is quite different from becoming a Bahá'í later in life when the use of alcohol had been routine. For many new Bahá'ís this is a huge lifestyle shift. Internalizing the law of abstinence from alcohol can take time. One can obey the law and still be at war inside. It is prudent for Bahá'ís from non-drinking families to be aware of how difficult a struggle abstinence can be for some new Bahá'ís and almost-Bahá'ís.

> Is there any Remover of difficulties save God? Say: Praise be God! He is God! All are His servants, and all abide by His bidding!
>
> *The Báb*[37]

'What do Bahá'ís think about homosexuality?'

Amongst the many other evils afflicting society in this spiritual low water mark in history, is the question of immorality, and over-emphasis of sex. Homosexuality, according to the Writings of Bahá'u'lláh, is spiritually condemned. This does not mean that people so afflicted must not be helped and advised and sympathized with. It does mean that we do not believe that it is a permissible way of life; which, alas, is all too often the accepted attitude nowadays.

We must struggle against the evils in society by spiritual means, and medical and social ones as well. We must be tolerant but uncompromising, understanding but immovable in our point of view.

The thing people need to meet this type of trouble, as well as every other type, is greater spiritual understanding and stability; and of course we

Bahá'ís believe that ultimately this can only be given to mankind through the Teachings of the Manifestation of God for this Day.

Written on behalf of Shoghi Effendi[38]

A number of sexual problems, such as homosexuality and transsexuality, can well have medical aspects, and in such cases recourse should certainly be had to the best medical assistance. But it is clear from the teaching of Bahá'u'lláh that homosexuality is not a condition to which a person should be reconciled, but is a distortion of his or her nature which should be controlled and overcome. This may require a hard struggle, but so also can be the struggle of a heterosexual person to control his or her desires. The exercise of self-control in this, as in so very many other aspects of life, has a beneficial effect on the progress of the soul. It should, moreover, be borne in mind that although to be married is highly desirable, and Bahá'u'lláh has strongly recommended it, it is not the central purpose of life. If a person has to wait a considerable period before finding a spouse, or if ultimately, he or she must remain single, it does not mean that he or she is thereby unable to fulfil his or her life's purpose.

The Universal House of Justice[39]

While recognizing the Divine origin and force of the sex impulse in man, religion teaches that it must be controlled, and Bahá'u'lláh's law confines its expression to the marriage relationship. The unmarried homosexual is therefore in the same position as anyone else who does not marry. The Law of God requires them to practise chastity.

Even though you feel that the conflict between sensuality and spirituality is more than you can bear, your affirmation – 'I do know I am a Bahá'í' is a positive factor in the battle you must wage. Every believer needs to remember that an essential characteristic of this physical world is that we are constantly faced with trials, tribulations, hardships and sufferings and that by overcoming them we achieve our moral and spiritual development; that we must seek to accomplish in the future what we may have failed to do in the past; that this is the way God tests His servants and we should look upon every failure or shortcoming as an opportunity to try again and to acquire a fuller consciousness of the Divine Will and purpose.

Written on behalf of the Universal House of Justice[40]

DIALOGUE

This conversation took place between two male college students:

Guest: 'So what do Bahá'ís believe about homosexuality?'

Bahá'í: 'Having a homosexual relationship is forbidden.'

Guest: 'Why? I thought your religion was open-minded; I'm surprised you'd be against gays.'

Bahá'í: 'The Bahá'í Faith is contemporary and that's why it appeals to so many people. But basic morality seldom changes. By the way,

we're not "against" gays. Gays are human beings with feelings too.'

Guest: 'My cousin's gay. He's a good guy. He
says he's been gay all his life. He was born that
way. If God made him gay, then how can your
religion forbid him from being himself?'

Bahá'í: 'There might be many reasons why people are gay – genetic, social, psychological –
who knows? The scientific jury is still out. Science and religion have to develop hand in hand
and we have a long way to go in understanding
homosexuality. I don't know why God "made"
your cousin gay, if He did at all. Why are some
people born blind, mentally handicapped or
just plain ugly? No one said life is fair; it's certainly not easy. Gay people in our society are
often treated unfairly by others. Life's loaded
with tests. Passing them, or striving to, is good
for our spiritual development; at least that's
what the Bahá'í writings say.'

Guest: 'Are you saying my cousin is gay as some
kind of cruel test from God? That's nuts, man!
So what's my cousin supposed to do? Ignore his
feelings and marry a woman anyway? He's not
interested in women!'

Bahá'í: 'There's always celibacy.'

Guest: 'Yeah, right! Like he's supposed to go
through life without having any sex at all!'

Bahá'í: 'Sex is a want, not a need. Sometimes it's a distractingly strong want but it's not essential to life, like food or air. You don't die if you don't get it.'

Guest: 'Speak for yourself!'

Bahá'í: 'The Guardian of the Bahá'í Faith said that people put an over-emphasis on sex. I'm sure you'd agree it's a prevalent subject in our society. What's important to note is that the law of chastity is not specific to gays. It's for heterosexuals too. A straight guy who is attracted to a woman he is not married to is expected to control his feelings and not act them out. Bahá'u'lláh says that a sexual relationship is only for a man and a woman who are married to each other. Bahá'ís are encouraged to marry but if someone doesn't, then yes, he or she remains celibate.'

Guest: 'Some churches marry gay couples. If my cousin married his partner then would the Bahá'ís accept him?'

Bahá'í: 'Bahá'ís will accept and love your cousin because he is a *person*. Gay, straight, Chinese, Polish, tall, short, those details don't matter. He wouldn't be able to have a Bahá'í wedding though, since that is only permitted between a man and a woman.'

Guest: 'If he married his partner in another church, would you recognize his marriage?'

Bahá'í: 'Some countries do recognize same-sex marriages but the Bahá'í Faith does not. If he wanted to become a Bahá'í, the Bahá'í teachings on homosexuality would be shared with him. Being a Bahá'í means not only recognizing the Prophet Bahá'u'lláh but also accepting and *obeying* all his teachings.'

Guest: 'I guess that means there are no gay Bahá'ís then, huh?'

Bahá'í: 'Not true. There certainly are gay and lesbian Bahá'ís.'

Guest: 'Why would anyone deliberately join a religion that opposes his sexual orientation?'

Bahá'í: 'When a person recognizes the divine station of Bahá'u'lláh, unusual things can happen. When one's spiritual homing device finds the mark it has been yearning for, the attraction is irresistible. It is the *soul* that is attracted, even if there will be some challenges ahead for the individual.

'I have a friend who moved to a city where there were only three Bahá'ís – two local gay men and one straight pioneer. Because many of the gay men's friends were gay, teaching the Faith initially occurred within the gay community. Eventually, there were nine Bahá'ís, enough to form the first Assembly. The Assembly consisted of the two pioneers and seven gay guys.'

Guest: 'That must have been weird for your friend!'

Bahá'í: 'I wish I could have been there! My friend is a really straight Persian guy. I don't think he'd ever had gay friends before. It was probably an eye-opener for him.'

Guest: 'So what happened?'

Bahá'í: 'He says they were not able to consult on teaching or planning a Feast or other stuff Assemblies do because the subject of homosexuality kept coming up. He says all they could do was say prayers and deepen on the station of Bahá'u'lláh. Then a transformation started to occur.'

Guest: 'What do you mean?'

Bahá'í: 'Gradually the overt behaviour changed, without anyone saying it should. Some of the men went through remarkable personal healings.'

Guest: 'Are you saying that if gays just pray enough, they won't be gay anymore? How crazy are you?'

Bahá'í: 'Some of the gay Assembly members resigned from the Faith. They had joined because their friends did, without fully realizing what it meant. They thought the Bahá'í Faith was a sort of social club. But some of the men did continue their lives as celibate gays, growing spiritually in their relationship with Bahá'u'lláh.

'Does prayer cure everything? I suppose God can change anything He chooses. We are advised as Bahá'ís to use both medical and spiritual forms of healing; to take advantage of the best that science has to offer *and* remember to turn to our Creator in humble prayer.'

Guest: 'I don't know, man. Praying to be "cured" from being gay sounds like a simplistic answer to a complex subject. Gays in our society have a really tough battle on their hands just because other people can't handle the fact that they're gay. If everybody, including religions, would just accept that 10 per cent of the population is gay and leave it at that, then we could all just get on with life.'

Bahá'í: 'I'm not trying to convince you that the Bahá'í writings are right and that you should agree with them. You asked what Bahá'u'lláh said about homosexuality and I told you. It's okay if we don't agree on this.'

Guest: 'Yeah, you're right. Our friendship is more important than arguing about this. Let's stay off this subject for a while.'

'Why can only Bahá'ís go to the 19 Day Feast?'

The 19 Day Feast is an institution of the Cause, first established by the Báb, later confirmed by Bahá'u'lláh and now made a prominent part of the administrative order of the Faith. These 19 Day Feasts are for the Bahá'ís, and the Bahá'ís exclusively, and no variation from this principle is permitted.

Written on behalf of Shoghi Effendi[41]

It can be explained, in a friendly manner, that the Nineteen Day Feast is an entirely private religious and domestic occasion for the Bahá'í community when its internal affairs are discussed and its members meet for personal fellowship and worship. No great issue should be made of it for there is certainly nothing secret about the Feast but it is organized for Bahá'ís only.

Written on behalf of the Universal House of Justice[42]

As regards your question concerning the Nineteen Day Feasts: this is really a matter of secondary importance, and should be decided by the Assembly; meetings which have been publicly advertised for a certain date cannot, obviously, be cancelled. As to non-Bahá'ís attending: this should by all means be avoided, but if non-believers come to a Nineteen Day Feast, they should not be put out, as this might hurt their feelings.

Written on behalf of Shoghi Effendi[43]

Regarding the Nineteen Day Feast, the principle universally applicable is that non-Bahá'ís are not invited to attend, and if you are asked about this you can explain that the nature of the Feast is essentially domestic and administrative. During the period of consultation the Bahá'ís should be able to enjoy perfect freedom to express their views on the work of the Cause, unembarrassed by the feeling that all they are saying is being heard by someone who has not accepted Bahá'u'lláh and who might thereby gain a very distorted picture of the Faith. It would also be very embarrassing for any sensitive [non-]Bahá'í to find himself plunged into the midst of a discussion of the detailed affairs of a Bahá'í community of which he is not a part. A non-Bahá'í who asks to be invited to a Feast will usually understand if this matter is explained to him.

Written on behalf of the Universal House of Justice[44]

DIALOGUE

This discussion took place at a fireside between a Bahá'í and her guest:

Guest: 'The 19 Day Feast sounds really neat! Can I go to one?'

Bahá'í: 'No, I'm sorry. The 19 Day Feast is only for Bahá'ís.'

Guest: 'Why? I've been to other things at the Bahá'í Centre. They were always open to the public. *Our* church services are open to everyone. Why can't I go to yours?'

Bahá'í: 'Because a Feast is more than just worshipping together. We also consult very openly about the affairs of the community. Yes, the public is invited to services at your church but can anyone just walk into a meeting of the church board? Can they make suggestions on how the church is run? Can they ask to see the financial records?'

Guest: 'No. Is that what you do at Feasts?'

Bahá'í: 'In part. A report of the local fund is shared and Bahá'ís are free to give their comments and advice. They are also encouraged to comment on any other matters they choose to and offer suggestions to the Assembly. The Bahá'ís need to feel free to speak openly without visitors present.'

Guest: 'What if I didn't say anything? I wouldn't bother anyone. No one should worry what I might think. I like the Bahá'í Faith! That's why I want to go. I could just sit there and listen. I just want to see how you consult.'

Bahá'í: 'If you and your husband were having a frank discussion about a family matter, say you had strong opposing views on how to raise your children, and then an unexpected visitor came to your door, what would you do? Carry on the discussion in front of the guest or save it for later while you turned your attention to being hospitable to your guest?'

Guest: 'Depends who it is! Usually we'd finish that conversation later.'

Bahá'í: 'It's the same in the Feast. If a non-Bahá'í were present, the Bahá'ís would put the comfort of the visitor ahead of their own feelings. Even if the visitor would be comfortable with everything being said in the Feast, if a Bahá'í didn't know that and withheld a comment for fear of the impression it could give to the guest, then that Bahá'í would be deprived of fully participating in the 19 Day Feast.'

Guest: 'Okay. That's fair. What would you do if someone accidentally came to a Feast, not knowing it was for Bahá'ís only?'

Bahá'í: 'If it was a small Feast in someone's home, then it would probably be turned into a 'Unity Feast'. We'd have the devotions and social time, skipping the administrative portion.

'In a larger community that might have a Bahá'í Centre with many rooms, someone could invite the visitor into a room other than where the Feast was being held and have a fireside with him. Why Feasts are only for Bahá'ís would lovingly be explained to the visitor without making a big deal about it. The visitor would be shown warmth and hospitality so as not to make him feel embarrassed for having walked in on a Feast.

'Our community has monthly Unity Feasts with all three Feast components – devotional, consultative and social. Would you like to go to one together?'

Guest: 'I'd love to!'

'But Jesus is the Son of God!'

This is not a question, as you can tell. It is, however, the response of many Christians when Bahá'ís inform them of the station of Bahá'u'lláh. It's often said in a tone suggesting that being the Son of God is the ultimate title a Manifestation can have and any other religious founder is inferior. It is as if to say, 'He's the Son of God. That's the end of it. No point in listening to any further information.' A Bahá'í will not always be able to convince a Christian friend of Bahá'u'lláh's station. He *can*, however, show his friend that a title such as 'Son of God' should not inhibit people from continuing open-minded spiritual investigation. The Bahá'í can demonstrate how he himself accepts Jesus as the Son of God as well as accepting the other Prophets.

DIALOGUE

One Bahá'í explained her understanding of the teachings about Christ this way:

Bahá'í: 'Bahá'ís accept Jesus as a Prophet, as well as Muḥammad, Moses, Zoroaster, Abraham and all the other Manifestations of God. We follow the teachings of Bahá'u'lláh because He is the most recent Manifestation and His teachings are applicable for today.'

Guest: 'Jesus wasn't a prophet. He was the actual Son of God!'

Bahá'í: 'Yes, Jesus was the "Son of God". He was also called the "Spirit of God" and "Christ". Muḥammed was called the "Seal of the Prophets". "Bahá'u'lláh" means the "Glory of God". Bahá'u'lláh has many other titles, including the "Supreme Manifestation" and the "Redeemer". But this isn't a contest to see whose name is bigger – the Son of God versus the Supreme Manifestation. I trust that people have the wisdom to actually study the spiritual teachings these Manifestations brought to mankind and not only focus on the titles by which they were known.'

Praying at Firesides

Remember Rita and Holly, the stressed-out fireside hosts in the previous chapter? Once their guest was settled into their living room Rita said, 'Prayers! Shall we begin with prayers? Do you like Bahá'í prayers? What do you want to do? Should we pray?' Although their guest went along, prayers weren't necessarily appropriate.

'What?' some Bahá'ís might say. 'Praying is always a good thing to do!'

Perhaps it is to a seasoned Bahá'í but not all people feel this way, especially if they have not prayed before.

On our first date, my husband, Sia, and I went for a walk in the Edmonton river valley. The path leads to some parts which are like a deep forest. At one point we stopped and sat on a bench near a stream. Keep in mind I was not a Bahá'í.

'Shall we say some prayers?' Sia asked me. We had already learned that we both practised prayer and meditation, so the suggestion did not seem odd.

'Okay,' I said. I went first.

'Dear God,' I started. 'Thank you for the nice day I'm having, thank you for my family, for the good friends I have' – and on and on I went with my 'gratitude list'. It was followed by a hearty 'Amen'. That was my prayer. That's how I had always prayed and it was the only way I knew. Then it was Sia's turn.

I don't remember which prayer he said. All I recall is thinking that the man had forgotten how to speak English. He was reciting some strange verses with a bunch of peculiar words like 'thee' and 'thou' and 'lovest'. I sneaked a look at him with one eye open, not believing what I was hearing. (Evidently I didn't hold it against him, as I did accept his invitation for another date and eventually marriage!)

If Bahá'í prayers seemed odd to someone like me who already enjoyed praying, imagine how Bahá'í prayers appear to people who are unfamiliar with prayer of any form. If you became a Bahá'í recently, you probably recall how you felt the first time you heard Bahá'í prayers read or recited. You may have thought they were beautiful, maybe you thought they were weird. If you grew up in a Bahá'í home, you might be puzzled as to how anyone could find prayers at all uncomfortable because they are so meaningful to you. It is for those potential guests who are not yet comfortable with praying that we use discretion when including prayers at firesides.

Bahá'ís, generally speaking, like to pray. We start our Assembly and committee meetings with prayers, we gather for dawn prayers, we even pray for no special reason, just because we're together and enjoy focusing spiritually with Bahá'í friends. We have only two occasions in our Faith when prayer is obligatory – a daily obligatory prayer and the prayer for the dead. There is no obligatory fireside prayer. Just because *you* might be accustomed to starting Bahá'í gatherings with prayers is not a justifiable reason to start firesides this way. Firesides are for non-Bahá'ís, not Bahá'ís. Think about the guests and what will make them feel most comfortable in your home. You might pray at your first fireside together; you might wait until the third or even the twenty-third meeting.

Treat every fireside as a new experience and introduce praying together when you believe it is appropriate for your guests. If you do happen to pray with someone who is shocked by Bahá'í prayers, it's okay. They'll get over it, just as I and many others did. And it will give you another topic for discussion!

6

Responding to Opposition

Fireside guests do not always agree with what they hear about the Bahá'í Faith. They can make comments like, 'Well, I still believe in reincarnation', or 'I think living together before marriage is good for a couple'. They aren't necessarily trying to convince you, the Bahá'í host, that they are right; they just need you to know where they stand. A person's beliefs are integral to who he believes he is. To have a shift in belief, or even to be considering one, can feel both exciting and threatening. When introduced to a new concept, a guest may want to think about it further when he is alone and not experience a transformation in front of others. Changing one's beliefs makes some folks uneasy, humbled that they may have been 'wrong' previously. Many people need to hold onto and defend their old beliefs for a while. This isn't bad. It shows how much they care and that they won't change their minds with every passing religious fad. There is no shame in growing; that's why we're all here. To supplant an old belief with a new and improved version is a healthy part of life. If a fireside guest appears unshakable in his position, which is different from the Bahá'í teachings, resist the temptation to conclude that this person will not embrace the Bahá'í Faith. Many seekers are their most obstinate just prior to declaring their Faith in Bahá'u-'lláh!

Donna is a good example. She and her husband Sam were investigating the Faith together. After a few months, he became a Bahá'í. Neither of them expected that they would join the Faith at the same time. They wanted to be clear that if they each became Bahá'ís it was not because the other one had done so.

The last waking hour of each day was their time for reading the writings. Donna immersed herself in Bahá'í books and was full of pressing questions. Each night she'd fire them at Sam. After all, he was a Bahá'í now and she hoped he could answer all her questions. One night Donna was particularly persistent.

'But *why* are the writings in such awkward English? And *why* can't I say "daughter" instead of "son" when I pray? And while we're at it, *why* can't I say the short obligatory prayer in the morning instead?' She unleashed every outstanding grievance that night. It was a long session. Sam answered to the best of his humble ability but it was quite clear to him that he would be the only Bahá'í in their household for quite some time, perhaps forever.

The next morning they went out to run errands together. Donna was in the car first, waiting. When Sam climbed into his seat he saw a piece of paper sitting on the dash in front of him. 'How could a

Some people can be very persistent

ticket get in here?' was his first thought. Then he looked closer. It was a declaration card. And it had Donna's signature on it.

'What is this?' he asked in disbelief.

'It's my declaration card,' she smirked.

'Your WHAT?' After the sleepless and exasperating night he had just had, this was the last thing he expected to see.

'It's my declaration card, silly. I'm a Bahá'í.'

'What was last night all about then?'

'Oh, I just had a few last details to sort out.' Donna had an irrepressible, contented grin.

It took a minute of silence for Sam to assimilate what he was witnessing. He didn't know whether to kiss her or choke her.

Donna was radiant.

Sam gave her a long, tender kiss.

Argumentative Guests

'Abdu'l-Bahá wrote:

> In accordance with the divine teachings in this glorious dispensation we should not belittle anyone and call him ignorant, saying: 'You know not, but I know.' Rather, we should look upon others with respect, and when attempting to explain and demonstrate, we should speak as if we are investigating the truth, saying: 'Here these things are before us. Let us investigate to determine where and in what form the truth can be found.'[45]

It is a beautiful fireside when neither the guest nor the host are bothered by their clash of ideas as they search for the truth together. Unafraid to have differences, they have a common goal. They share their points of view with mutual respect and courtesy.

Not all firesides go so smoothly, unfortunately. The worst fireside nightmare for many Bahá'ís is that of having a guest disagree with some aspect of the Faith and become loud and argumentative. If the guest is a friend of the host, the likelihood of this happening is small, unless the guest has poor manners and minimal coping skills. When the guest and host do not know each other well, or when the fireside is held in a meeting room and not in a Bahá'í's home, aggressive people may become more courageous. An argumentative guest may fire up because of his attachment to his beliefs and he feels threatened when the Bahá'í teachings do not support them.

When someone is agitated and verbally aggressive, calming him down becomes a challenge. The situation is even more embarrassing for the host if there are other guests present. What can you do if, God forbid, this scenario occurs in your living room? Here are some useful communication tools:

1. Don't argue with him. That would be pouring gasoline onto a fire. Even if you make a strikingly good point, an agitated guest is not about to give you credit for it. What is most important to you at that precise moment – proving you're right or restoring peace in your home?

Don't argue with me!

In her book *A Manual for Pioneers*, Rúḥíyyih Khánum states:

> We must not argue with other people. Occasionally I have found that during the question period in my lectures someone begins to dispute with me; when I find we are about to have an argument I say, 'Argument is forbidden in my religion, I have no desire to argue with you, you are quite free to hold your own views and I to hold mine.'[46]

2. Address the behaviour. You could say, 'When you're standing up and shaking your finger at me, I can't focus on what you are saying and I really want to hear what you have to say.' If he raises his voice or pounds his fist on the table, draw his attention to it and tell him how it makes you feel. He may not even be aware he's doing it. This shows the guest that *how* people speak with one another is more important to you than competing in a religious debate.

3. Speak quietly. Even whisper. Whispering has a stunning effect on people! When someone is shouting and is met with a whisper, it will often stop him cold. I'm a nurse in a busy Emergency Department of an inner-city hospital and I use whispering almost daily with drunk or belligerent patients. It's harder for someone to shout while he's being whispered to. A bully wants you to push him, even verbally, so he can come back at you with a bigger punch. Staying calm is the best way to diffuse him.

If I were to shout to an agitated patient, 'Stop swearing and kicking the wall or you'll be thrown out of here!' you can bet his next words will also come out at top volume.

I will often walk up close to a ranting and raving patient, smile and whisper, 'Hi. My name's Catherine. What's yours?'

'John,' he replies. In a whisper!

'How can I help you, John?' still whispering.

'I've got this cut on my head! I got hit with a pipe. I'm bleeding, man!'

'That must hurt. Let's clean it up and see if you need stitches.'

The conversation can be over before the patient even realizes that he, too, is whispering!

Maria Montessori, the founder of the Montessori teaching method used in many private schools today, taught the value of whispering. If students became too talkative and weren't paying attention to her, she would whisper instead of raising her voice to them. Soon the students would realize they might be missing something interesting and would then listen keenly, even hushing other students who were still talking.

With a loud fireside guest, a whisper is often the fastest route to cooling him down. It may be as simple as saying his name until he becomes aware of the contrast in your volumes.

'Jim – Jim – Jim,' you whisper.

Eventually he stops.

'I'm not comfortable with people yelling at each other in my home,' you say, still in a whisper.

He regains his composure.

4. Maintain his dignity. Once someone realizes his behaviour has been inappropriate, sudden embarrassment can set in, especially if others are present and you, the host, remained patient during the outburst. Give your guest a dignified exit from the conversation.

'I understand you feel very strongly about this issue. You know so much about (blank) and I look forward to learning more about it from you next time.' Then move the conversation on and include other guests. If *you* protect the bully's ego, he won't need to preserve it himself with more shouting and trying to prove his worth.

5. Watch your body language. When someone is arguing in a raised voice, it has an effect that makes the other person want to respond in kind. Resist your body's urge to raise your eyebrows, open your mouth ready to retort, hold a finger in the air or to sit on the edge of your chair. Waiting patiently and lovingly for the person to finish says more than your spoken words.

The other fireside guests are watching you. If one guest is having a struggle, the others can see that for themselves. They will be more impressed by your Bahá'í courtesy and refusal to argue than any clever retort you might have.

Moderation

At an International Bahá'í conference held in Tirana, Albania, in 1995 Rúḥíyyih Khánum told an audience of hundreds that when she is being interviewed by the press she doesn't worry about all the 'important' things she could tell them about the Bahá'í Faith. Instead, she emphasized that she tries to leave them with a high regard for the Bahá'ís.

'Leaving a good impression is most important', she told us, 'because people probably won't remember what you said.'

There is so much we want to tell our fireside guests about this wondrous Cause of Bahá'u'lláh, especially if they are showing keen interest. A challenge for Bahá'í hosts is not so much what to say in a fireside as what *not* to say. After your guests have left, don't run after them down the driveway calling, 'Wait! I haven't told you about the administrative order yet!' Exercising restraint and not overloading one's guests with information can be a test to an enthusiastic Bahá'í.

Bahá'u'lláh reminds us:

Not everything that a man knoweth can be disclosed, nor can everything that he can disclose be regarded as timely, nor can every timely utterance be considered as suited to the capacity of those who hear it.[47]

Good advice for fireside hosts.

How people speak to one another is important

7

Bahá'ís at Your Fireside

Bahá'ís at Firesides

When should a Bahá'í be present at another Bahá'í's fireside? Unfortunately, many a fireside has been spoiled by a Bahá'í who really shouldn't have been there. Simply put, the fireside is not an open social event for Bahá'ís to attend, though some Bahá'ís act as though it is.

One evening at our Bahá'í Centre, another woman and I were in the kitchen washing dishes after a Feast.

'What are you doing tomorrow night?' she asked me.

'We're having a fireside,' I said.

'Oh good!' she exclaimed. 'What time will it be? Maybe I'll come!'

I put the dish cloth down and paused for a moment. I had to think of a kind response and yet I was disturbed that she assumed she could appear at our fireside uninvited.

'We're having our neighbours over for supper,' I said. 'It will be their first fireside. Do you think you and I could visit some other time?'

'Okay!' she chirped.

I had protected my fireside but I don't believe the Bahá'í friend understood I was protecting it from her. Our guests and this Bahá'í had little in common. My husband and I had new neighbours who knew we were Bahá'ís. This dinner would be the first occasion we would talk about the Faith in depth. I doubted our neighbours would so openly discuss their spiritual quest in front of this stranger, even though she was a Bahá'í.

I suspect my Bahá'í friend assumed that our fireside was the 'evening-presentation-everyone-invited' kind. That may have been the only kind of fireside she knew. Now braver and wiser, if I were back in that conversation again with her, I would lovingly explain to her why so many firesides are small and private.

If you met a friend on the street and she mentioned she was on her way home to cook supper, I doubt you would seriously say to her, 'I love supper! What are you cooking? I'm going to eat at your house tonight.' If one would no sooner invite oneself to supper at another person's home in this manner, why do it for a fireside? It's simply rude to assume you may attend someone else's fireside if the host hasn't invited you.

The believers are entirely free to hold as many little teaching groups or Firesides as they please in their own homes privately. No one has a right to intrude in another person's home uninvited. In fact this personal, informal, home teaching is perhaps the most productive of results.

Written on behalf of Shoghi Effendi[48]

'Open-door' Firesides

Some Bahá'ís do have 'open-door policies' on their firesides. They have let it be known that anyone may attend any of their firesides. Often they are held on the same day of each week and the hosts even advertise. We *can* consider ourselves invited to this kind of fireside. Still, it is a courtesy to inform the host of one's intention to attend. I do wonder about the motive of the visiting Bahá'í, though. If she is not bringing a guest and is only going for her own pleasure, she has forgotten for whose benefit firesides exist.

Bahá'ís who regularly have small firesides on a set day of the week may still be very carefully choosing those they invite. Some are very artful in their skills of entertaining, including how they mix their invited guests, including Bahá'ís. Sensing the social group within which a seeker would feel most receptive to the Faith is part of their planning. It would be a shame for an insensitive Bahá'í to barge in on such a precious setting.

Before I became a Bahá'í, I went to firesides at several people's homes. There was one hostess with whom I felt a special rapport. She was a person with whom I could trust my most private concerns about the Bahá'í Faith – questions that I wasn't going to ask just anybody.

She had an open-door policy for her firesides. Sometimes six people would come, sometimes none. One evening there was only the hostess and myself. The hostess asked me if there was anything in particular I would like to know about the Faith. I told her I had a list of miscellaneous questions I'd written down while reading books loaned to me by Bahá'ís. She smiled warmly and said she'd be glad to do her best at answering my questions. I pulled out my paper and we began. It was such a relief to finally be discussing these issues that were gnawing at me.

After half an hour there was a knock at the door. The house was small and I could hear the conversation between the hostess and the person at the front door.

'Hi! I was just driving through the city when I remembered you have firesides on Wednesdays, so I thought I'd drop by! It's so good to see you! We haven't seen each other for months!' said the man at the door.

Pleased to see an old Bahá'í friend, the hostess invited him in. We were introduced and he was served tea. The next 20 minutes of conversation comprised the two Bahá'ís catching up on each other's news. 'Where have you been? How are you doing?' and so on. Eventually they turned back to me.

'Now, where were we?' said our hostess, ready to resume our discussion.

My list was already folded and tucked away in my pocket. I was not comfortable divulging my insecurities before this boisterous stranger, the same stranger who had showered the hostess with attention and had only delivered a few obligatory greetings my way.

No one ever really knows what another person is thinking but I'm going to make a rather safe guess in this situation. As the visiting Bahá'í was driving through the city, I doubt his thoughts were, 'Hey! There's a fireside happening tonight at (blank's) house! There might be seekers there! I have to go and help! I want to teach the Faith!' His behaviour didn't suggest that teaching me the Faith was his motive that night. He wanted to visit a Bahá'í friend and knew he could find her home on Wednesdays because of her firesides.

Go ahead and have an open-door policy for your firesides if you want to but be aware that those who show up may not be to the best benefit of your invited seekers. *The purpose of the fireside is to share the Faith with non-Bahá'í guests.* Bahá'ís can and should meet their social needs elsewhere.

Community Firesides

Many Bahá'ís say they have neighbourhood or community firesides. People living in the same area agree to hold firesides together. 'If no guests come, then we just deepen,' they say. Sadly, they have missed the point of firesides. Picture eight Bahá'ís showing up at a 'fireside' with no guests. If you're not bringing a guest, then why on earth are you going to a *fireside*? To watch? Hoping someone else brings a contact? To socialize? To deepen yourself?

The passage from Shoghi Effendi quoted in Chapter 2 describes a fireside as being an event 'where new people are invited', one which 'will bring the knowledge of the Faith to more people', and 'enrich its circle of friends, and finally its members'. The fireside is our way of proclaiming and expanding the Faith. Nowhere does the Guardian say that a fireside's purpose is for Bahá'ís to meet their own needs to deepen or socialize.

If a Bahá'í is not serving a clear purpose for the benefit of guests at a fireside, then he need not be there. If you like the deepening aspect of firesides when no guests show up, then organize real deepenings in your neighbourhood. And plan firesides that are truly focused around non-Bahá'í guests.

A Bahá'í community in a small town recognized it was in the 'community fireside' trap. One member explained, 'When our Assembly decided we would have weekly firesides (one home was volunteered), we all thought we had to attend to show our support. Sometimes we'd have guests, sometimes not. But there were always six to eight Bahá'ís.'

They came up with a creative solution. A host family would invite one guest or couple for dinner or evening coffee. They made personal invitations that ensured guests would come. Another community member would provide a dessert, another would help

the host with house cleaning and another family
would care for the host's children. It was a team effort
and it worked! They did this for each Bahá'í household in their town. By sharing the workload, every
fireside had guests and the Bahá'ís had more free
time because they weren't attending every fireside.
Best of all, the Bahá'ís no longer out-numbered their
guests.

Too Many Bahá'ís

Having more Bahá'ís than guests at a fireside is an
error worth preventing. A fireside is not for the benefit of the host's ego. If one can boast 'I had 15 people
at my fireside yesterday!' but 12 of them were
Bahá'ís, that's not something to be proud of.

Non-Bahá'ís still investigating the Faith, as well as
some Bahá'ís recalling their pre-Bahá'í days, have
shared stories of attending firesides where they were
the only seekers. One woman recounts,

> At my first fireside there were five Bahá'ís and
> myself. No one told me that all the other people
> were Bahá'ís; I had to figure that out for myself as
> the evening went along. I felt like they were all
> looking at me. Several times I was asked if I had any
> questions. I didn't. I just went there to listen that
> night. I wanted to observe what goes on at a fire-
> side. But I could feel everyone staring at me, as if
> they were waiting for me to ask something pro-
> found. It made me really self-conscious! In hind-
> sight, now that I'm a Bahá'í, I realize that they were

It seems the Bahá'ís came to the fireside just to watch

simply excited to have a seeker at their community fireside. Some of them just came to watch. I learned from that experience never to let that happen at a fireside in my house.

Think about it. Would *you* like to be the only seeker at a fireside stacked with Bahá'ís you didn't know?

Another Bahá'í was also the minority guest at a fireside when she first investigated the Faith. This is her story:

It took almost an hour before I realized I was the only seeker present amongst six Bahá'ís. There was so much talk going on between these Bahá'ís who knew each other well, I didn't have the chance to speak. I could have interrupted with a question like, 'Excuse me – I know this isn't the topic you're talking about but would you mind if I asked a few unrelated questions?' I didn't have that kind of courage.

I thought that creating the environment in which the seeker could ask questions was the *host's* job, not the seeker's! I knew the host. I liked her. But who were all these other people? I was invited to a fireside, so I was told. I felt like I was an extra person at a Bahá'í gathering. They used unusual insider words I didn't know, like 'Alláh-u-Abhá', and that made me feel uncomfortable.

I hoped these extra Bahá'ís would eventually go home so the host and I could talk. For most of the evening she was too busy in the kitchen or serving others to sit and talk with me. By 10:00 p.m. I was the last guest there and tired.

As I put on my coat to leave, the hostess finally asked me, 'Do you have any questions?'

'Lots,' I smiled. 'But I have to go. I work early in the morning.'

She smiled back. She was a lovely hostess and the supper was delicious but I didn't go back to that home for another fireside.

Now don't assume that the hostess was inexperienced at giving firesides. In fact, the opposite was true. She was a veteran Bahá'í, respected as a successful teacher of the Faith. The error we sometimes make once we are well-rehearsed and comfortable with having firesides is that it then becomes more challenging for us to see our firesides through the eyes of our non-Bahá'í guests. Do we say 'Alláh-u-Abhá' to Bahá'ís present, despite the Guardian's warning about such behaviour?[49] Do our guests feel outnumbered by Bahá'ís, rendering the guests a silent minority? Have we truly planned our fireside around the benefit and interests of the non-Bahá'í guest(s)? That Bahá'ís leave a fireside saying it was good means nothing. The fireside wasn't for them.

When there are more non-Bahá'ís than Bahá'ís at a fireside, the non-Bahá'ís are more likely to speak. If they have a response to another non-Bahá'í's question or comment, they will voice it. Watching fireside guests teach the Faith to one another is an exhilarating experience for the Bahá'í host! You'll deny everyone that experience if you put too many Bahá'ís in the room. The Bahá'ís know what the writings say on various subjects. If they speak too soon, everyone misses out on the non-Bahá'ís trying to work it out together. When there are too many Bahá'ís, the non-Bahá'ís are also less likely to speak, fearing that what they say might be 'wrong' – they don't want to look foolish in front of the Bahá'ís, who to the non-Bahá'ís appear more knowledgeable about religion.

The Guardian tells us that 'Each must hold a Fireside in his or her home, once in 19 days'. Bahá'ís who attend other people's firesides, even if they bring guests, or Bahá'ís who attend 'community' firesides should perhaps ponder on these words of the Canadian National Teaching Committee:

> A fireside is your personal responsibility. Other Bahá'ís should be present only if invited by you. You may wish the assistance of other Bahá'ís and of course should feel free to invite them. However, the intimacy of the small group should be preserved and the guests should not be overwhelmed by Bahá'ís. Nor should other Bahá'ís attending your fireside feel they have fulfilled their own personal duty for holding a fireside – they should also have their own.[50]

'They should also have their own.' Enough said.

Firesides Not at Home

The question is sometimes raised whether a fireside held in a Bahá'í Centre, a community hall or other rented room, such as on a university campus, is a fireside. After all, it's not in a Bahá'í's home. Certainly, it's a fireside. You are hosting guests, providing hospitality, creating an environment which exudes Bahá'í warmth and love to invited seekers. The goal is to facilitate dialogue about the Faith. But this kind of fireside, or participating in a neighbourhood fireside, does not exempt the individual believer from his responsibility to host his own firesides.

Attending Another Bahá'í's Fireside

We have established that each Bahá'í should be having his own firesides, that Bahá'ís should not dominate firesides and that we should not attend someone else's fireside without his clear invitation. Let's look at some occasions when it *is* appropriate for a Bahá'í to attend another Bahá'í's fireside:

1. You're bringing a guest. You may have a contact whom you feel would benefit from meeting a certain Bahá'í. You call him, describe your relationship with your contact and ask if the two of you could attend a fireside at his home. He may include you in an already scheduled fireside or set up a private appointment for you.

2. You're the guest speaker. That's a good reason to attend!

3. You have been invited for variety. The hosts might have a few regular guests and feel it's time they met Bahá'ís other than themselves. We had a group of four seekers coming every two weeks to our home. One day we asked another Bahá'í to join us.

She eloquently answered questions using different phrases and examples than we had. It was a refreshing experience for all of us!

4. You're a new Bahá'í. Once someone enrols in the Faith, we don't kick him out of the fireside, saying, 'You're a Bahá'í now! Go off and start your own firesides!' Becoming a Bahá'í is a beginning, not an end. New Bahá'ís usually like to stay a part of the group, however large or small, that facilitated their transformation. As they become integrated into the Bahá'í community, they naturally wean themselves from the fireside where they discovered Bahá'u'lláh.

There are various arguments for attending other people's firesides for the purpose of 'learning to give firesides'. I have met rural Bahá'ís who have enrolled in the Faith without ever having met a Bahá'í. They discovered the Faith through reading books, recognized that the Faith was for them, and contacted the national office or a Bahá'í listed in the phone book of the nearest city. Such people have never been to a fireside. If they ask to attend someone else's fireside to see how that person does it, that curiosity is understandable.

Such new Bahá'ís could have an advantage, though. If they only have the teachings on firesides as their guide and simply invite friends in to visit with the intention of mentioning the Faith, they can have anxiety-free firesides. Their firesides won't be big productions. If they visit other Bahá'ís and see them arranging more structured discussion group firesides, I hope the new Bahá'ís will see this as just one kind of fireside and not the 'right' kind.

Some dear folks, despite their awareness of the writings, still need mentoring until they can stand on their own and hold their own firesides. Their shyness and fear of teaching disables them. By partnering with a more confident Bahá'í, who sheds love and compassion on the less secure friend, the new Bahá'í can find his God-given strength. The two can hold firesides together, alternating between their two homes, until both are successful teachers.

Bahá'u'lláh assures us that with His assistance we shall be victorious:

> Arise to further My Cause, and to exalt My Word amongst men. We are with you at all times, and shall strengthen you through the power of truth. We are truly almighty. Whoso hath recognized Me will arise and serve Me with such determination that the powers of earth and heaven shall be unable to defeat his purpose.[51]

Lousy Guest Speakers . . . It Can Happen!

Another way a Bahá'í can ruin a fireside can come from a most unexpected source – the guest speaker. Here are a couple of examples.

A travelling teacher was coming through our city and needed accommodation for two nights. We offered our home. Coincidentally, one of those evenings we already had an 'evening discussion group' fireside booked in our home and the traveller offered to be our guest speaker. This was something we had not yet tried with this particular group of seekers. We called the five expected guests to tell them they were in for a real treat – a special guest would address them that evening. The speaker had lots of experience and came highly recommended. We had no reason to suspect what would actually happen that night.

The speaker asked us to select from one of four topics he was presenting on this tour. We did and he gave a very educational presentation that evening. It was full of colourful stories that exemplified his points well. Everyone enjoyed it – for a while. But the speaker wouldn't stop. He talked on and on. Finally he took a large breath and asked for questions. But before a seeker was finished asking his question, the speaker began to reply with a very long-winded answer. While enjoying his own answer to the question, the speaker would remind himself of yet another story and on he talked. This happened several times.

At one point, a seeker who didn't have a question wanted to share with the others something interesting he had read. 'You know,' he said, 'in *Thief in the Night* I read that – '

'*Thief in the Night*!' said the guest speaker. 'Let me tell you a fascinating story about *Thief in the Night*!' He was off again.

The five guests, my husband and I all looked around at each other uncomfortably. I felt embarrassed for our speaker. Everyone except the speaker could see what he was doing. He was totally unaware of his behaviour and how he was perceived by the group. All his training and preparation had not included how to listen to others. There is a wisdom in letting fireside guests do most of the talking.

Finally I had to interrupt. 'Excuse me, but I believe Gordon (the non-Bahá'í) was telling us something about *Thief in the Night*. What were you saying, Gordon?'

The guest speaker stopped, slightly flushed, and let Gordon finish. The moment Gordon was done, the speaker continued.

I'm sad to say, this was the pattern for the whole evening.

These were experienced fireside guests who had never witnessed such behaviour from a Bahá'í before. Bahá'ís aren't perfect, I know. But I felt responsible and embarrassed because it was happening at *my* fireside.

The other disaster happened during our year-long pioneering stay in Albania. A very deepened Bahá'í was visiting from another European country and we were asked if we could set up some deepening and fireside appointments for him. We did.

A deepening with 16 Albanian Bahá'ís was arranged. It was to be a full-day meeting. We all sat in chairs in a circle in a rented room. The speaker, a kind, loving and very deepened man, spoke while looking down at the floor. He seldom, if ever, made eye contact with his audience. He did pause appropriately for translation.

Choose your guest speaker with care

His voice was monotone. The content was too deep for this novice audience. After an hour people were nodding off to sleep. At the lunch break more than half of the audience left, not to return. During lunch, my husband and I were consoling each other in the corner – half embarrassed, half laughing at our predicament. If we hadn't been the hosts, we would have escaped at lunchtime too! Once again we had a guest speaker who made absolutely no assessment of his audience or how he appeared to them.

Late in the afternoon, after his day-long mono-logue, the speaker finally said to the remaining partic-ipants, 'Do you have any questions?' Of course the room was silent! Questions about what? That blur of words that lost the audience's attention long ago?

My husband, Sia, a professional teacher and a very engaging presenter, was sitting next to the speaker. Sia leaned over and gently said to him, 'You need to ask them a more specific question, like 'Would this last point about holding youth deepenings work well for your community?' The speaker did this. Finally, the participants became involved in a discussion and everyone's attention increased.

The point I'm making here is that just because someone is from out of town he is not necessarily a good speaker. The same is also true of local Bahá'ís who offer to speak. Being knowledgeable on a subject *does not* mean one knows how to communicate it well to others. The successful speakers I've had at firesides and classes for new Bahá'ís have been people I've first seen giving presentations at other events and I have confidence in their communication skills.

For the sake of your guests, if you are considering having a speaker whom you have not seen before, you have the right, even *responsibility*, to inquire about his abilities. References will usually tell you how knowledgeable a speaker is. Dig further. You want to know if he is interesting to listen to and watch. At least speak with the proposed guest speaker on the phone before booking him. If he has any behaviours that concern you in that conversation, such as interrupting, that's a signal that it could happen in your fireside too. If anything in that interview makes you feel uneasy about having that speaker at your fireside, investigate further. Follow your gut feeling as to what is best for your contacts.

I have been to some fascinating talks given by people I've never heard of before and was glad I had brought guests. As Bahá'ís we all wish this could happen every time. The reality is, though, luck with unknown speakers is random.

In Chapter 11 we will look at some basic presentation skills to help *you* give engaging talks that won't leave your audiences snoring in their seats.

8

Inviting People into the Faith

Hoping to be Invited

Jean was attending firesides regularly. She liked the teachings of the Bahá'í Faith and accepted Bahá'u'lláh as a Prophet of God. She enjoyed the company of the Bahá'ís she knew and they enjoyed hers. They could always count on Jean to come to their firesides. Their firesides were always a success, the Bahá'ís believed. Even if no one else came, they knew Jean would always be there.

For more than a year Jean and her Bahá'í hosts covered nearly every subject imaginable in their monthly visits. All felt enriched by the spiritual discussions and reading the holy word together. They had become good friends. Jean looked forward to her spiritual oasis in the Bahá'í home.

But Jean had one question she withheld. It was 'Can I join the Bahá'í Faith?' Jean had the impression that the Bahá'ís were an established group into which she should not invite herself. Surely if she were permitted to become a member she would have been told so by now.

It was not until a visiting Bahá'í attending the same fireside one day, impressed by Jean's closeness to the Faith, asked her outright if she'd like to become a Bahá'í.

'Yes, I would!' she responded. Jean was overjoyed by the invitation. Finally, she was 'in'!

Her hosts were speechless. I'm not sure what shocked them most – how up-front the visiting Bahá'í was, the fact that Jean had said yes or that it had not occurred to *them* to invite her much earlier. Jean was certainly ready. I suspect those Bahá'ís had not yet mentally accepted the possibility of people actually becoming Bahá'ís at their firesides. They had been raised in Bahá'í families and had never witnessed someone enrolling in the Faith before. Declarations and expansion of the Faith only happened in other places, they thought.

In its Riḍván Message of BE 153, the Universal House of Justice in paragraph 18 states that we foster the advance in the process of entry by troops 'first by spiritually and mentally accepting the possibility of it'. Do we accept that seekers can and will enrol in the Faith through our firesides? If Shoghi Effendi says that 'The most effective method of teaching is the Fireside group', then we must prepare ourselves for the fruits of these firesides.

Most Bahá'ís want to share the Faith with other people. If someone is showing interest, we are eager to tell them all they wish to know about the Central Figures, the principles and so on. But all too often we stop there. We provide information about the Bahá'í

teachings and neglect to invite the seeker to join the Cause. We must remember that Bahá'u'lláh's healing message is good for *all* humanity. We must enable others to embrace this Cause. Some Bahá'ís are magnificent spreaders of the revelation of Bahá'u'lláh yet have never crossed the threshold to directly invite someone into the community of the Greatest Name.

Jean is not the only Bahá'í to recount how long she waited for an invitation to become a member of the Bahá'í community. Ron hopped from fireside to fireside in several towns over several years. He travelled frequently with his work and wasn't a regular guest at any particular fireside. Every few months he would show up again and the Bahá'ís were glad to receive him. None of his hosts ever ventured to invite him into the Cause. Seeing him so rarely and being unaware of Ron's rotating exploration of the Faith, no one ever thought it was his place to invite him. Fed up with wondering, it was Ron who took the initiative and one day asked if he could become a Bahá'í.

I hope you never have a Ron or a Jean go unnoticed at your firesides. The onus should not be on the guest to initiate discussion on how he enrols in the Bahá'í Faith. Be unapologetic. Courageously invite people into the Cause!

Becoming Audacious

During the time I was practising being courageous in inviting people into the Faith, I received a phone call from a stranger. He said he had been up all night reading Bahá'í literature he had found on the Internet. He called the local Bahá'í Centre and someone there had given him our phone number. I asked him if he'd like to attend our fireside at the weekend, go to a Unity Feast next week together or drop by that evening. He chose to come by that same evening.

When my husband came home from work I announced, 'Hey, guess what! We're not going to a movie tonight after all!' He looked disappointed. We had both been looking forward to our movie date. I told him about the phone call and that we were having a fireside in a few hours. Sia was pleased. No movie date compares with holding a fireside.

The man arrived and told us all the discoveries he had made on the Internet. He had found Gloria Faizi's *Introduction to the Bahá'í Faith* and read it all late one night. His excitement wouldn't let him sleep. He had heard of the Bahá'í Faith years ago; now he was reading about it on his computer. He expressed that all that was left for him to do was now meet some real-life Bahá'ís.

'Does discovering the Bahá'í Faith feel like "coming home" for you?' I asked him.

'Yes!' he said.

'Do you think you're a Bahá'í?' I asked.

'Yes!' he said eagerly, moving to the edge of his seat.

My husband was caught off-guard by my direct question to this first-time visitor.

'But you don't have to decide right now!' he said. 'You can sleep on it, if you like.'

'Oh, okay,' said the visitor, taking this comment as advice.

Having the afternoon to prepare mentally for the visit, I had decided that if this seeker seemed ready to be invited into the Faith, I would venture into new territory and ask him. The fact that this would be our first meeting didn't matter. A ready soul is a ready soul.

The mistake I made was not sharing my new bravery with my husband. We discussed domestic details during supper and didn't plan the fireside together. No wonder he was surprised by my new behaviour. Until that day our joint approach had been to invite people into the Faith gradually, encouraging them to fully investigate.

After our guest left I told my husband that lately I had been thinking of being more audacious in my teaching approach and inviting people to become Bahá'ís. That night the perfect opportunity had presented itself. It felt peaceful and right to pose the invitation to this seeker. It was confirmed by our guest's affirmative response. (He enrolled after our next fireside together.)

My husband embraced this new teaching approach. We made a pact that from then on we would look for opportunities to invite seekers into the Cause, including those people we may have previously overlooked.

Phrasing the Invitation

The words we use when inviting someone to become a Bahá'í have an effect. The phrases we choose could attract or repel him.

Anne was visiting the home of her Bahá'í friend. The two women were chatting over tea in the Bahá'í's apartment when another Bahá'í who lived across the hall knocked and walked in. The two neighbours were accustomed to being this casual with each other. The neighbour stayed for tea.

The three women talked openly about the Faith. Anne was obviously well-read and was a good friend of the Cause. At one point the Bahá'í neighbour, known for being rather uninhibited, leaned over to Anne and grabbed her arm saying, 'So why aren't you a Bahá'í? You know so much about the Faith already!'

Anne graciously brushed away the question, as well as the fingers penetrating her arm. When recounting this story to me she said she was bothered by the *negative* in the question. 'Why *aren't* you a Bahá'í?' She said that had the question been phrased with more sensitivity, she would have been willing to discuss the current status of her religious investigations.

'Why *aren't* you a Bahá'í?'

'Why *don't* you become a Bahá'í?'

Questions phrased with built-in negatives seldom elicit positive responses. They may make the listener defensive, formulating an 'I'll tell you why not' response. A warmer, non-attacking question is usually better received.

'Would you like to become a Bahá'í?' asked with a smile is often enough. The person knows she is welcome and the decision remains respectfully hers.

An invitation I like to use is, 'Are you a Bahá'í?' (Could you be a Bahá'í? Is it possible you are a Bahá'í?) It suggests to the friend that being a Bahá'í is a matter of *recognition*, not so much a decision. Shopping for a religion is not the same as shopping for a pair of shoes, where one tries on several kinds, then buys the best available. The revelation of Bahá'u'lláh has power inherent within it. Either a seeker feels it resonating inside him or he doesn't. When a seeker recognizes that he believes in the teachings of this Faith, and that he may well have for a long time, and then learns there is a word for his beliefs – 'Bahá'í' – he is relieved of making a decision. It is merely a recognition and acknowledgment of that which he inherently knows to be the truth.

Some people are thinkers. They accept the Faith through their intellect and reasoning. They come to love Bahá'u'lláh later. Such a person may respond well to 'Do you think you are a Bahá'í?' or 'Do you think Bahá'u'lláh's blueprint for society is the answer?'

In 1960 Hand of the Cause John Robarts was teaching the Faith to Don Rogers.

'Will you join the Bahá'í Faith, Don?' he asked him.

'No thanks,' Mr Rogers said. 'I'm not a "joiner".' He liked the Bahá'í Faith and enjoyed associating with the Bahá'ís. But joining a group of any kind was not his style.

'But Don,' replied Mr Robarts, 'we need you *now*.'

That did it. Admiring Bahá'í principles was not enough. Don Rogers needed to know he was needed. For a new World Order to spread throughout the planet and be implemented, dedicated individuals are required.

Don Rogers became a Bahá'í. He and his wife Barbara held firesides in their home in Saskatoon that were historic portals for many others to join the Cause. In 1985 he was appointed to the Continental Board of Counsellors. His years of service as a Counsellor included serving at the International Teaching Centre at the Bahá'í World Centre in Haifa until 1998. Thankfully, Mr Robarts extended that poignant invitation.

There is no one correct way to invite people into the community of the Greatest Name. Trust your judgement and remember the Concourse is with you. If you are open to opportunities for inviting people into this glorious Cause, they will come to you.

Enrolling in the Faith

A less direct method for inviting someone to become a Bahá'í is to explain to the seeker how one becomes a Bahá'í. In our firesides Sia and I say to our guests something like the following:

When becoming a Bahá'í in Canada, one fills out an enrolment card which is sent to the National Spiritual Assembly. The bottom of the card reads: 'I accept Bahá'u'lláh as the Messenger of God for today and apply for membership in the Bahá'í Faith.' The enrolment card enables the National Assembly to know how many Bahá'ís are in Canada. The new Bahá'í will start receiving *Bahá'í Canada*, a national community magazine, in the mail. A person is then permitted to attend the 19 Day Feasts, vote and donate to the Fund. The use of the enrolment card is purely administrative. Being a Bahá'í is truly a personal spiritual matter – between the individual and Bahá'u'lláh.

Having offered this explanation, we give the seekers enrolment cards. Often we tuck the cards inside books they are borrowing, saying, 'In case you want this someday, you now have one.' Ninety per cent of the cards come back to us filled in, be it days, weeks or even months later. Once someone's soul recognizes Bahá'u'lláh, it's just a matter of time before the signature follows.

We also explain to them that becoming a Bahá'í is truly as simple as it appears. There are no exams to pass or ceremonies to endure. If we don't make jokes about initiation ceremonies, the guests do!

'There's the head-shaving ritual but we were saving that news for later!' Firesides can be playful.

Not every country uses enrolment or declaration cards to register new Bahá'ís. Find out what method is followed in your country and use that. The point

Explain that becoming a Bahá'í is simple

is not the method itself but that the seeker knows how to enrol in the Bahá'í community.

'I'm not good enough to be a Bahá'í'

Many 'almost-Bahá'ís' describe their hesitation about enrolling in the Faith even though they undoubtedly believe in Bahá'u'lláh. They say they couldn't be as upstanding and perfect as the Bahá'ís they know. They don't feel worthy of being Bahá'ís. They say they couldn't possibly live up to the standards of moral and righteous living set out in the writings.

It is important to assure someone at this crossroad that being a Bahá'í does not mean one is a perfect example of 'living the Bahá'í life'. Quite the opposite. We take all our human frailties along with us and continue to strive to improve our character *within* the Bahá'í Faith. A very wise friend, Dr Riḍván Moqbel, who wrote the foreword for this book, once said, 'Being a Bahá'í doesn't mean we have "arrived". It simply means we have agreed to go.'

Requirements for Enrolment

There are humorous stories of travelling teachers opening new areas and feeling overwhelmed by the swiftness with which some people, even groups, will ask to enrol in the Faith. After a short explanation of the Bahá'í teachings, their listeners say they want to be Bahá'ís! The travelling teachers say, 'But wait! I haven't told you all the laws and principles yet!' Should they accept these enrolments or not?

No human being can judge whether or not another's heart has truly been inspired by Bahá'u'lláh or whether he genuinely accepts Him. We can, however, ensure that the seeker realizes that the Bahá'í Faith isn't a social club or association. Becoming a Bahá'í is a matter of religious conviction.

The Universal House of Justice in a letter of 13 July 1964 clarified the conditions to be met when enrolling in the Faith:

> The prime motive should always be the response of man to God's Message, and the recognition of His Messenger. Those who declare themselves as Bahá'ís should become enchanted with the beauty of the teachings, and touched by the love of Bahá'u-'lláh. The declarants need not know all the proofs, history, laws, and principles of the Faith, but in the process of declaring themselves they must, in addition to catching the spark of faith, become basically informed about the Central Figures of the Faith, as well as the existence of laws they must follow and an administration they must obey.[52]

The seeker needs to be basically informed about the Central Figures and of the *existence* of Bahá'í laws and an administration. Knowing all the details is not an initial requirement. As teachers, we try to give seekers as much information as we can without overwhelming them. If an inspired soul wants to rush to join the Cause, we should not discourage him. The above statement of the House of Justice gives us the means to ensure a minimum requirement is met. If *after* becoming a Bahá'í a person discovers finer details like his country already has a National Spiritual Assembly or that Bahá'ís fast for 19 days or that they don't drink alcohol, that is okay. If he was taught properly, by becoming a Bahá'í he has accepted that there are laws and an administration that must be obeyed, whatever they be.

'Welcome!'

Between birth and death there are a few major landmark events in one's life – graduation, marriage, having children, etc. Declaring one's faith in Bahá'u-'lláh is one of those pivotal events. It is not a decision arrived at lightly or frequently. So when someone becomes a Bahá'í at your fireside, or when you meet a new Bahá'í, congratulate him! Acknowledgment of this major event in one's life is usually appreciated.

Whenever appropriate, I like to say, 'Welcome home.'

'Yes!' is often the reply. 'That's exactly what it feels like. I've come home.'

'Welcome to the Bahá'í community!' is also a safe and loving welcome.

As long as Bahá'u'lláh needs instruments for His Cause, we have a mandate to invite people into the Faith. The Blessed Beauty wrote:

> Through the potency of the Name of the Best-Beloved, invite thou the receptive souls unto God's holy court, that perchance they may not remain deprived of the heavenly Fountain of living water.[53]

9

Building Your Library

The Gift

You have a guest in your home and she's showing interest in the Faith. Now what? GIVE her something! Give her a book or booklet she can take home.

The magazine *The Bahá'ís* is perhaps the best teaching tool yet printed. It is an 80–page glossy magazine-style booklet, with photographs on every page and brief write-ups on most aspects of the Faith. It's a colourful synopsis of the Bahá'í Faith, which has proved to intrigue its readers. *The Bahá'ís* is a favourite first gift given to many seekers.

If your contact already has *The Bahá'ís* magazine, there are other good gift choices. A little prayer book, the *Hidden Words*, *Gleanings*, a compilation on consultation, or whatever feels appropriate, taking into consideration what the two of you have discussed and where her interests lie. Many Bahá'ís keep a collection of new books just for these occasions. These books are not displayed on their library shelves; they're often stored safely, preserving the books' new condition as gifts.

The same guest doesn't need a gift at each of your firesides she attends. That could get quite expensive! It would also diminish the meaning of the gifts. Too many gift books could easily become part of a growing collection of unread material in the seeker's home. One gift, however, is usually treasured and read.

Experienced teachers of the Faith also keep a supply of books reserved as special gifts for the occasions when seekers become Bahá'ís – prayer books, daily reading books or other special books. Adding a little inscription like 'Welcome into the worldwide fellowship of the Bahá'í community!' or another thoughtful phrase can be added with love.

I still own and cherish four books that were given to me by Bahá'ís who warmly welcomed me when I formally acknowledged I was a Bahá'í. Still today when I pick up these books, I remember the moments when they were given to me and how I appreciated the loving welcome extended to me. The Bahá'ís who gave me the books may have forgotten those exact moments now but I never will.

Books for Sale

I'd like to share with you a lesson I learned from some fireside guests. I would not have had the courage to initiate these events on my own.

A woman borrowed a copy of *Gleanings* from us. After two days she returned it. Knowing she hadn't read it all, I encouraged her to keep it longer, saying I had another copy.

'No, thanks,' she replied. 'I don't like borrowing books. These are the holy writings of Bahá'u'lláh. I'd prefer to buy my own copy.'

The copy I had loaned her *was* brand new. She paid me for it and was happy to keep her new book.

A few weeks later the same woman came to a fireside where four other people were present. She had previously requested that the day's discussion be on Bahá'í consultation. The other guests were aware of her suggestion and agreed to this.

I had chosen a few passages to study from the booklet *Consultation: A Compilation*. A few hours before the fireside was to begin I was struck with an idea. Instead of making unattractive photocopies of a few quotations for everyone, I thought it would be better if each guest could follow along from the booklet itself. It would look classier and show each guest a sample of a Bahá'í publication. (This format was a break in tradition for us. Our firesides are usually much more casual). Trouble was, I only owned one copy of this compilation.

Knowing it was a common and well-used compilation, I hurriedly phoned nearby Bahá'í friends and asked if I might borrow their compilations NOW. Once I had six loaners arranged, I jumped in the car and drove around making pick-ups. I promised each Bahá'í I would return the booklets promptly and in good condition.

The fireside went very well. Towards the end, the same woman who had bought *Gleanings* stated that she would like to buy a copy of the consultation compilation. She asked which book stores in our city carried it. None, was the answer. (That's an issue our Local Spiritual Assembly has since remedied. We recently secured a 'Bahá'í Books' section in a local book store.) Telling her to wait a couple of weeks while I ordered one for her didn't feel right. She was ready for it *now*. I already knew that borrowing my tattered copy was not what she wanted.

One of the copies I had borrowed from a Bahá'í friend was brand new, never used by him. I sold it to her! Telling my Bahá'í friend that he would have to wait two weeks until I replaced his booklet would be easier for me to live with than keeping the seeker waiting. The next day I told the Bahá'í why I sold his booklet; he was delighted that it was in the hands of a seeker.

That incident prompted me to order six copies of the consultation compilation the next morning. The deepening went so well that Sia and I decided to have copies of the compilation on hand should we want to try the same kind of fireside with another group of guests. I also ordered other books to add to our Bahá'í library. The box of books happened to arrive on the day of a fireside with the same five guests. I opened the box in front of them and showed them the new additions to our library, in case they'd like to borrow some new books. They bought them!

The ease with which they pulled out their cheque books and chose the Bahá'í books they wanted to buy taught me a lesson. Some people are prepared to buy books when they are not comfortable borrowing.

Borrowing carries an indebtedness. People have to remember to return the items. But if they buy books, they can keep them. The buyer has also made an investment. The indebtedness is now to oneself to read the book. Most people feel more compelled to read a book they have chosen and paid for themselves than one that has been suggested and loaned to them.

Thanks to those fireside guests, I now have no hesitation in showing people our lending library *and* a selection of the same titles for sale.

The Lending Library

There is an old adage, 'Never lend anything you're not willing to give.' In lending, the possibility always exists that the item will not be returned. For some elusive cosmic reason, this is especially true of books. Books often do not find their way home again. If you have a precious book, say a leather-bound-first-edition-autographed-copy-of-whatever, and the thought of losing it makes you think 'detachment' is a dirty word, don't lend it. It's okay to have a 'Reserve' section in your home library – books that can be enjoyed on the premises but not taken away.

A wise Bahá'í builds his own lending library. These are books not for *you* to read but to lend to your guests. You may not plan to read *Bahá'u'lláh and the New Era* again for a while. You've read it twice and you've bought a pile of new Bahá'í books you are eager to get into. But you keep a copy of *Bahá'u'lláh*

and the New Era, even two or three copies, because it's a good starter book for fireside guests. By having multiple copies of popular books, you will, it is hoped, have one available whenever a seeker asks for it.

If a fireside guest shows interest in a given subject, it's a shame if you have to say, 'I know of a book you'd really like! If you wait two weeks, I'll get it by mail order!' It's a missed opportunity, especially if the book is a common one you wish you owned anyway. I'm not suggesting you have a complete Bahá'í book-store on hand. There are, however, some books Bahá'ís say they lend most frequently. Your lending library might include:

> *Gleanings from the Writings of Bahá'u'lláh*
> *The Hidden Words*
> *Tablets of Bahá'u'lláh*
> *Selections from the Writings of 'Abdu'l-Bahá*
> *Some Answered Questions*
> *Bahá'u'lláh and the New Era* (Esslemont)
> *The Bahá'í Faith: Emerging Global Religion*
>   (Hatcher and Martin)
> *Thief in the Night* (Sears)
> *The Family Virtues Guide* (Kavelin/Popov)
> prayer books
> videos

Bahá'ís also frequently loan compilation booklets on a variety of subjects. A small booklet often seems less daunting than a large book. When the booklet is returned, the seeker may be ready for something longer.

Where Did that Book Go?

I've watched my home library shrink. I lend books, believing I'll remember who has what. Months pass. Sometimes 12 or more. Now where are my books? I can remember only a few overdue villains. I phone them.

Their responses vary:

'So sorry! I'll get it back to you right away!' And they do.

'So sorry! I'll get it back to you right away!' And they don't.

'I loaned it to (blank). Try calling her.'

'What book?'

Once a loaned book has been on someone else's shelf or night table long enough, another strange book phenomenon kicks in. The borrower believes he owns it. He's had it so long, it *must* be his. He can't quite remember where or when he bought it, he's just certain he did. Despite the fact that my name and phone number are penned inside the cover (where he hasn't looked), the book is now his!

My stray books are my responsibility. Or so I tell myself if I ever want them back. I now keep a library log. It's a little notebook in which I write the borrower's name, the title of the book and the date borrowed. It's okay, too, if the borrower sees me making these notations. It reaffirms his part of the 'contract' to return the book eventually. After, say, six months have passed, I call the borrower and ask,

'How are you enjoying *The Revelation of Bahá'u'lláh*? Are you ready for the second book in that series?' It's a gentle way of reminding him that he still has my book.

If someone asks, 'Are you sure *I* borrowed it?' I can say, 'Yes, I have it written here, "Barry Doe, *The Revelation of Bahá'u'lláh*, Book One, loaned on April 6th".' Who can disagree with that? My written notes versus his unsure memory. After looking through his books, the borrower usually responds with, 'Oh, yes, you're right. I've got it here.'

Half of our 'library customers' are Bahá'ís, usually wanting reference books. The lending period on such books is short, since they are in high demand, usually by my husband and me. We both have an uncanny knack of lending the exact book the other needs to prepare a talk.

'Honey, where is *Lights of Guidance*? I need it for tonight.'

'Funny you should ask. Jill came by just this afternoon and borrowed it.'

Sigh. Marriage is so humorous.

10

After the Fireside

The Evaluation

After you have held a fireside, give it a little evaluation. Evaluating doesn't mean judging harshly. We tend to be our own toughest critics. When your guests have left, very *tenderly* evaluate your own fireside. Review what you think went well and what you'd like to do differently in the future. With each fireside you'll learn things that will make your firesides better and better.

You might ask yourself questions like:

- Did I prepare well enough?

- Did I make time to pray beforehand?

- How were my presentation skills? (If you gave a talk.) For tips on improving your public speaking skills, see Chapter 11.

- Did I invite guests who benefited from being together?

- Should the fireside have been smaller or larger for certain people?

- Was serving chocolate fondue too messy and distracting?

'Did my guests get what they needed?' is often too difficult a question to answer. We can easily be wrong when trying to evaluate how someone else experienced a fireside.

My friend Val says that on the occasions when she feels she gave a poor fireside, meaning she wasn't pleased with her explanations about the Bahá'í Faith, these are often the times when her guests call her the next day to say how thankful they are for her helpful insights! She has long given up trying to guess what her guests think of her firesides. Val just makes a point of staying at home the evening *after* a fireside; that's when she tends to receive most calls from her fireside guests.

Carol and Mansour had two firesides with guests who didn't know each other. They had invited two men and one woman. These were the only interested seekers they knew, so inviting them all on the same dates seemed like a good way to have a fireside. On both occasions the two men asked questions and shared their opinions. The woman stayed quiet, answering briefly if directly spoken to. This puzzled the Bahá'í hosts. The woman guest was a well-educated colleague of Carol and her hosts were certain she would contribute richly to the discussion about the Bahá'í Faith.

Carol called the woman the day after the second fireside and said, 'I sensed that last night was not the best forum for us to have a good chat. Would you like to come again without other guests here so that just the three of us can talk?'

The woman accepted. The next week she returned for a private fireside with Carol and Mansour. The friend had been reading Bahá'í literature and amazed her hosts with her understanding of complex passages. Without the other guests present she felt comfortable speaking her mind freely.

Before the evening was over, she signed an enrolment card.

Three cheers for Carol and Mansour's evaluation of their firesides. Not because their friend became a Bahá'í but because they recognized that one of their guests might not be having her needs met and they phoned to follow up. They offered her an alternative and she took it. She *was* ready to declare her faith. She just needed a few private questions answered first. Enrolling in the Bahá'í Faith was something she wanted to do and she felt best doing it privately with the friends who had taught her the Faith.

If another Bahá'í has been part of your fireside, be it your spouse or a friend, you can help each other with the evaluation. Asking questions such as 'Did I talk too much?' or 'How would you have answered that question about fasting?' gives you feedback from a fellow Bahá'í.

It's also pleasing to have someone with whom to share the post-fireside joy. Having a great fireside often leaves my husband and me speechless. As we close the door after the last guest leaves, there are no words to describe how rewarded we feel. We usually just stand there in silence for a few minutes, sharing a hug and quite frequently a 'high-five'.

If you've held your fireside on your own, you may feel inspired to call a close Bahá'í friend.

'I've just had a wonderful fireside! Can I tell you about it?' Victories are lovely gifts to share.

When evaluating one's own firesides, the small and casual firesides usually get the best marks. The more we try to 'stage' something big, the harder the task becomes, increasing the potential for the host's disappointment.

The Nurturing

After the fireside, it is important to nurture the relationship with your guests. This is when you invite them to Unity Feasts, Bahá'í holy days or other events. You invite them to another fireside. You introduce them to other members of the Bahá'í community. During the nurturing phase it is important to get back to them with answers to questions they have asked, which you were unable to answer during the fireside. At a fireside it is completely acceptable to say 'I don't know' to questions; in fact, people actually admire it. It shows that you're human and aren't trying to be a know-it-all. Saying 'That's a really good question! I'll need to look it up. Can I get back to you about that?' gives you an opportunity to speak with the guests again about the Bahá'í Faith. You can share your findings with them over the phone the next day or offer to get together again. You can say 'I've found that quotation we were searching for the last time we were together. It's in a wonderful book called *Selections from the Writings of 'Abdu'l-Bahá*. I'd be happy to bring it over to you.'

Several Bahá'ís attending the *Successful Firesides* Workshops have voiced their hesitation to phone friends of the Faith who haven't shown any interest in becoming Bahá'ís. The contacts may have even stated that they do not intend to become Bahá'ís. Yet they continue to come to holy days and other events when invited. Bahá'ís want to nurture these relationships. We need to have friends of the Faith. Some Bahá'ís feel awkward making calls to these people, inviting them to yet another Bahá'í function. One workshop participant said, 'I called a woman recently who said to me, "I know why you're calling. You're going to ask me to come to a Bahá'í thing, aren't you?"' The Bahá'í was embarrassed. 'How can I continue to share the Bahá'í Faith with this woman without feeling like I'm bothering her?' she asked.

The answer is straight forward: Be a friend. Call her for reasons other than Bahá'í meetings. Call just to go for a walk together. If she is ill, offer to do errands for her. Living the Bahá'í life and being of service to others often teaches more effectively than taking the guest to an organized meeting. Being a friend also extends to those seekers who *are* actively pursuing the Bahá'í Faith for themselves. Seeing each other socially or having phone chats without necessarily talking about the Faith strengthens a friendship. To call only to invite someone to Bahá'í meetings can make one look and feel like a pushy salesperson.

In small towns where the expansion of the Faith is discouragingly slow or sometimes even non-existent, there have been cases of the few local Bahá'ís fixing on an individual who has shown some warmth towards the Cause. Overwhelming guests with copious invitations to Bahá'í gatherings has put some contacts off. A loving balance of attention is needed.

Megan, a Bahá'í, lived in a small city. At a holy day gathering Megan met Barb, the guest of another Bahá'í. Discovering they had a lot in common, Megan asked Barb if she'd like to come to her home for a visit. A few days later they had lunch together. Soon after, Megan received a phone call from the Bahá'í who had brought Barb to the holy day event.

'Why are you trying to steal my contact?' snapped the Bahá'í.

'What?' asked a baffled Megan.

'Barb's *my* contact. I met her first!'

'Can't she have more than one Bahá'í friend?' asked Megan.

A strange but true conversation. Megan was innocently and naturally befriending someone who was interested in the Faith. The jealous Bahá'í had not had many teaching opportunities recently and saw her one and only contact slipping away into the dining room of another Bahá'í with whom she had more in common. Introductions like these are to be celebrated! Barb could indeed have both Bahá'ís as her friends. If she continues her search, hopefully Barb will come to know several people within the Bahá'í community quite well. I sincerely hope that the two Bahá'ís involved in this incident worked out their differences without Barb becoming aware of the battle over her friendship.

Letting Go

I heard a Bahá'í lamenting that a friend of his wasn't showing much interest in the Faith. 'He'd make such a great Bahá'í!' he said, genuinely sorry that his friend was showing no signs of joining the Faith.

The writings of Bahá'u'lláh are much like an oasis in the desert. If you are walking through a desert, refreshed from your stop at an oasis, and you see someone searching for water, you will gladly indicate to him where you found water. Whether he goes that direction or not remains his decision. We can tell the world that God has sent another Messenger, in fact a Supreme Manifestation, but what people do with that information is beyond our control. It can be disheartening for a Bahá'í to watch a friend pass up the Bahá'í Faith but we must detach ourselves from the outcome of our teaching. Bahá'u'lláh does say that He has given every person the capacity to recognize Him:

> He hath endowed every soul with the capacity to recognize the signs of God. How could He, otherwise, have fulfilled His testimony unto men, if ye be of them that ponder His Cause in their hearts.[54]

A person can have more than one Bahá'í friend

Bahá'u'lláh has given us the obligation to teach His Cause. He does not hold us responsible, however, for what others do with the news of His revelation. They may accept or reject His claim. You have not been mandated to forcibly save another's soul nor will you receive a commission cheque for 'making another Bahá'í'. You're just obliged to teach. Trust the Word of God to look after the transformation within people's hearts.

When a Bahá'í introduces the Faith to a friend and that friend becomes keenly interested in investigating Bahá'u'lláh's teachings, sometimes the Bahá'í holds a secret hope that he will be the person to whom the seeker first declares her acceptance of Bahá'u'lláh. Witnessing and supporting another person's discovery of the Bahá'í Faith, right through to her declaration, is exhilarating and rewarding to the Bahá'í teacher. In reality, however, that Bahá'í might only facilitate part of the seeker's journey. When tending the garden of a seeker's heart, you might plant the seed of Bahá'u'lláh's message, while another Bahá'í nourishes it with the waters of friendship. The seedling may sprout into a devoted seeker at your fireside or at someone else's. Later you might hear she blossomed into a declared follower of the Cause at yet another fireside. If the Bahá'í and seeker are close friends, yes, often the first teacher is the person to whom a new follower of Bahá'u'lláh declares her acceptance. Not to have expectations in teaching, though, is occasionally an exercise in detachment for Bahá'ís. Whatever role you play in someone else's discovery and acceptance of the Bahá'í Faith, rejoice that there is now another soldier for this mighty and triumphant Cause!

11

Presentation Skills

When you're visiting with a friend or sharing a meal, do you write down what you're going to say? Do you both read the conversation from a prepared script? Of course not. Friends will casually chat for hours without needing to look at any notes to guide them through their next words. This book has emphasized that firesides can be as simple and comfortable as any other conversation you have with your friends. What you know about the Bahá'í Faith can be shared with the same ease as discussing any other interest in your life. Bahá'ís are capable of having stress-free monthly firesides by keeping them small and informal.

You might already be an accomplished veteran of the small fireside. Perhaps you sometimes hold larger firesides in your home and are even asked to be a guest speaker at other firesides.

This chapter focuses on public speaking skills that will help you look and feel at home in front of an audience. Whether you are addressing a fireside of 10 guests or 100, or making a presentation at a 19 Day Feast, you too can benefit from learning some public speaking basics. Good public speakers are not born, they are made. They *learn* public speaking techniques and they practise them. So can you.

Even if you do not anticipate being a guest speaker at a fireside, by reading these tips you become aware of what goes into public speaking – what happens 'behind the scenes' for the presenter – and you will see how methodical it is. By reading these techniques, you will be aware of some valuable dos and don'ts, which you may unexpectedly need one day!

Does the thought of public speaking make you nauseous? Do you think you can't do it? If you had never played badminton before and were suddenly encouraged to try, you would want to find out a few things first – what the lines on the court mean, how to hold the racquet, how the scoring is counted and so on. Then you'd hit the birdie around a few times to see how much power is required to get it over the net. You'd be more comfortable playing a game with this background knowledge. It is the same with public speaking. People shouldn't be expected to just get up there and 'do it'. There are some basic rules to play by that help both you and your audience enjoy your presentation more.

Some people are actually attracted to public speaking in the same way that others are attracted to risky sports, such as sky diving. One *can* be afraid of something and still be willing to do it, even drawn to it. One prepares as best one can, then proceeds. By studying both the physical and psychological components of public speaking, one can learn what to expect and how to respond.

Silence

Have you ever been speaking in public and forgotten what you wanted to say? The fear of 'going blank' is most people's public speaking nightmare. They are afraid to stand in front of an audience, with all eyes staring at them, and having no memory of what they want to say next. There is actually a simple solution.

Silence is okay. Experienced speakers aren't afraid of silence. They even use it to their advantage. I frequently walk away from a lectern where my cue cards are to move around the room or to get closer to the audience. If I forget where I am in the presentation, I don't panic. I have choices:

1. I can pause until I remember where I am in the talk. What feels like an eternity to a nervous speaker is really just a brief pause to the audience.

2. I can return to the lectern and look at my notes.

3. I can joke with the audience and say, 'What was I just talking about?' It gets their attention as they test themselves to see if they were listening. Someone always shouts out what was last said. 'Thanks!' I'll say. 'I wish I was listening as closely as you are!' They laugh and the talk continues. Audiences appreciate seeing speakers being human and vulnerable. It gets them on the speaker's side.

Pausing when you forget your place in a talk is un-intended silence. Learn to be comfortable with it. Refreshing with your notes for a moment and then

Prepare for your presentation

proceeding confidently is preferable to appearing lost and stammering aimlessly. If you get flustered, the audience is embarrassed for you. If you appear relaxed, it is relaxed. Take the time you need before continuing.

Silence should also be planned into a talk. Allowing time for silence is just as important as choosing the words that you'll say. Pausing briefly now and then allows listeners to digest what was just said. A speaker who talks without pausing loses the attention of his audience. Minds wander in the drone of the speaker's voice. Pauses add emphasis. Not speaking and just looking at the audience for a moment says, 'This is important. Listen up!'

Voice

What does your voice sound like? If you're like many people, you don't like the sound of your own recorded voice. Nonetheless, in private, try recording yourself speaking or reading, then play it back. As your own worst critic, you'll be the first to notice annoying flaws, such as 'I hate the way my voice goes up at the end of every sentence!' Once you've become aware of potentially annoying habits, you can work on correcting them.

If you can't bear to record yourself, then ask a relative or good friend for feedback. If he knows this is a serious part of your preparation to give a talk, it is likely he will be honest with you and not just flatter. Someone with whom you have a trusting relationship will have the courage to tell you when you speak too quickly, too softly, or if you make unnecessary noises like 'um', 'uh', 'like' and 'you know'.

The improvements most people find they need to make are:

1. Slowing down
2. Lowering the voice
3. Pausing instead of saying 'um'

When you are quoting from the writings and your group is small enough such that microphones are not required, let participants read quotations aloud for you. Voices other than the main speaker's voice give variety to the presentation.

Body Language

The well-known research of Dr Albert Mehrabian demonstrated that 55 per cent of communication is what we see and 38 per cent is what we hear while the actual words used comprise only 7 per cent. If this is so, you will want to be acutely aware of what your body is saying! Here are three points to watch for:

1. Posture

Look at your normal posture in the mirror. If you have a tendency to slouch, try standing tall, with your shoulders back and head held high. Chances are this will feel exaggerated and phony to you. But look! In the mirror it looks good! Get used to how it feels. This is how you want to stand in front of your audience. How you *wear* your own body says more about you than the clothing you put on it. Poor posture is unattractive. Good posture, however, suggests self-esteem. The audience will enjoy the presentation more if it believes it can have confidence in you. So maintain good posture for the duration of your talk, even if this feels foreign to you.

2. Smile

An expressionless face on a speaker can imply that he isn't sure of his material. That makes an audience uneasy. A good presenter smiles a lot. It tells the audience 'You can trust me. I'm comfortable presenting this material to you.' The audience then relaxes and enjoys listening. The speaker may actually feel like he is smiling excessively. But it looks correct from the audience's point of view and that's the view that counts.

Audiences also have their own body language. Unfortunately, their smiles are an unreliable gauge of their enjoyment of a presentation. Some people tend to frown when they are concentrating on something they want to hear. Some remain expressionless even when they enjoy a joke. This can be interpreted as disapproval by the speaker, when that isn't the intention of those in the audience at all.

A speaker's preferred audience is one that leans forward, smiles and nods in agreement. This lets the speaker know he's doing okay and his audience is with him. But truthfully, you may only have one or two people who actively listen this way. The rest are just staring at you and you're not sure how to read them. The rule to go by is this: If they are still looking at you, you are probably doing fine. If several people in your audience are no longer making eye contact with you – they are gazing around the room, looking down, doodling, talking to someone beside them, nodding off – it is likely they are bored and it's time to go to your closing remarks.

3. Avoid Causing Distractions

Nervous speakers sabotage their own presentations by doing things that annoy and distract their audiences, such as jingling keys or coins in their pockets. The nervous speaker isn't aware that he's doing it but his audience is very aware. It's creating noise and the audience isn't listening to the speaker. Instead, people stare at the speaker's moving pocket, wondering when he's going to stop jingling. The easiest solution to this is to have your pockets empty. If you don't need an item for your talk, don't take it up there with you. A tissue in case of a sneeze may be all one needs. I was distracted by a speaker who twirled a pencil around his fingers throughout his entire talk. He didn't even use the pencil in his presentation! I sat on my hands, resisting the urge to walk to the front of the room and snatch the pencil away from him so we could focus on his speech instead.

It's all right to be nervous before or during speaking. It happens to all of us at some time or another. This is when a speaker can say to himself, 'I'm nervous. It's okay to be nervous. When I'm nervous I jingle my keys in my pocket. I've left my keys in my briefcase to prevent this. I'll stay conscious of what my hands are doing. I have my cue cards if I need them. I'm going to be just fine.' Being aware of his nervous behaviour and not allowing it to manifest itself in front of the audience gives the speaker a feeling of calm and control and gives the audience the same impression.

Hand gestures are a useful way to punctuate a talk. They add emphasis and sometimes drama. Too much hand talk, however, distracts from the spoken word. Excessive gesturing in front of one's own face leaves the audience wishing you'd simply put your hands down so people can see you. Gesturing while not speaking, such as while searching for the right words to say, is overly distracting. The audience wants to tell your hands to 'Shut up!' Unless you are signing to a deaf audience, let your hand movements accentuate your talk and not take centre stage.

Walking about in front of an audience is usually good. It gives people's eyes something to follow. People pay closer attention when a speaker moves towards them or looks at them. Pacing in front of an audience, though, is distracting.

I used to pace, until a friend pointed it out to me. I was 'test-driving' a talk in front of her one day.

It's all right to be nervous before a talk

'Do you know you keep walking back and forth in the same spot?' she indicated.

'Do I really?' I asked.

'Yes,' she said. 'Do that same section over again.'

Sure enough, as I talked I was taking three steps forward then three steps backward on the same section of carpet the entire time. I thought I was engaging the imaginary audience by moving towards it but by doing so in the same spot I was simply drawing attention to my feet. The next evening when I gave the talk to an audience of 50 people, I stood still more often. When I walked, I moved towards different parts of the audience. This enabled the audience to focus on what was being said and not on my pacing pattern.

Whether the speaker sits or stands also sends a message. In some cultures, to stand when others are sitting suggests the speaker is superior or thinks himself so. If the gathering is a small living room fireside, then sitting like everyone else is most appropriate. Sitting in a circle, if the room permits it, demonstrates equality and inclusion of all present. The rule to go by when deciding whether to sit or stand is generally this: if people cannot see or hear you well when you sit, then you stand.

If the meeting is large enough to have you on a podium, standing is in order. Unless you are Bill Cosby, few presenters can speak while simply sitting on stage and remain engaging. (A podium, by the way, is the raised platform on which a speaker *stands* and the item onto which he sets his notes is a lectern).

For long presentations I take a guitarist's stool with me. I don't like to hide behind a lectern and the stool gives me a central point to speak from occasionally. I can wander towards an audience and come back to the stool for variety of presentation. The stool is the right height for me to lean my derriere on, with one foot on the footrest and the other on the floor. I can casually continue the dialogue with the audience, walking again towards them without drawing attention to me getting on and off the stool.

Paper Handouts

Handouts can be useful aids during presentations. They give your audience a visual memento to accompany your talk. The *timing* of passing out pages to a small audience is what determines whether or not the handouts will be a distraction. When you hand out sheets of paper to people, they are going to look at them *immediately*. Be certain this is what you want them to do. During the *Successful Firesides* Workshop I use handouts. Before passing them around, I give clear instructions on how to do the exercises, where each group will meet, what time to return and so on.

On occasions when I have slipped up and given the handouts ahead of the instructions, the predicted behaviours have happened. People read their pages as soon as they receive them and tune out the verbal instructions. This results in a room of confusion when it is time to move into the break-out groups. So hang onto your handouts until you really want people to read them!

For large gatherings, say 50 or more, handing anything out during the meeting is usually time-consuming and distracting. Handouts can be set on chairs before the audience arrives.

Handouts are even useful at small informal firesides. Guests appreciate receiving copies of quotations you have shared. Being able to read along is often preferable to being read to. One or two quotations in a border on attractive paper makes a lovely keepsake. Provide just a little written information. If it is too lengthy, it will get thrown into the 'I'll read it some day' pile, which may be never.

Attire

How to dress for hosting or speaking at a fireside is actually influenced by the size of the fireside. For a small fireside in your home, it is better to be dressed down compared to the way you anticipate your guest(s) will dress. If you dressed up and your guests appeared in blue jeans, they might think, 'Oops, we're underdressed for the occasion!' and feel awkward. Putting one's guests at ease is every fireside host's goal and dressing casually or semi-casually can help. Of course, clarifying the dress code with the guests at the time of the invitation will alleviate guesswork on everyone's part.

If the gathering is medium-sized, say eight or more guests, the host should dress slightly up compared to the guests' dress code. If you are a guest speaker for a medium or large fireside, always dress up. If the dress code is casual, be semi-casual. If the occasion is semi-casual, then you wear semi-formal attire.

Wear clothing that fits well and feels good and you don't need to worry about. If you frequently have to adjust your garment or are concerned about how it looks, then *you'll* be distracted from your talk. And wear comfortable shoes. If you're to be on your feet for any length of time, you deserve to be comfortable. If you are comfortable, you can give your talk and your audience your full attention.

Reading Speeches

Beginner speakers will often type their talks out and read them word by word. This is not only unnecessary, it is uninteresting. The audience knows they are being read to and not spoken to. The tone of the average person's reading voice is less captivating than the voice of that same person genuinely speaking to the audience. If the speaker needs to look down at his notes for most of the time, the audience's attention easily drifts away. If you're not looking at the people, they're not motivated to look at you either!

A principle recognized in the arena of public speaking is that a speech should only be read in four specific settings:

1. Legal The talk being presented is a legal document or has legal consequences.

2. Political The event is a political one.

3. Ceremonial Social and religious ceremonies where the text is pre-determined.

4. Media If media are recording your speech.

The above four settings are occasions when the specific selection of words can be crucial. A slight error or paraphrase could have serious consequences. These situations warrant delivering a carefully prepared speech.

Given that we are discussing firesides here, we may therefore conclude that reading a word-for-word speech is neither necessary nor appropriate. That isn't to say that you may not *prepare* a word-for-word speech, however. The process of writing a talk is one way that many people commit the material to memory. It's like writing a grocery list. At home you decide what you will need from the store and write a list. The list goes into your pocket and you go to the store. If your list is short, you may find yourself going up and down the aisles, putting the needed groceries into your basket without ever referring to the list. If the list is long, chances are you can still gather most of your groceries without using the list. So if you feel more assured to stand before an audience with a fully prepared talk, that's fine. But *keep your eyes on the audience*. Your speech is there to anchor you if you need it. Many people feel comforted knowing their speech is in their hands, even if they seldom refer to it.

Cue Cards

Once you trust yourself not to need a verbatim speech with you, you'll find planning your speech much easier and faster if you use cue cards. Many public speakers use 3 x 5 inch file cards because they can be used discretely. And if you are holding onto them, they don't flutter the way a large piece of paper does in a nervous hand.

You will design your cue cards the way that best helps you remember what you want to say. Some people use diagrams called mind-mapping. Others write down the outline of their talks, just listing the headings of sections and the segues connecting them. If you have names, dates and other facts included in your talk, write them on your cue cards. Then you can spend your preparation time focusing on the overall concept of your talk and not memorizing the smaller data. If in the 'long version' of your talk, be it in your head or on paper, you have some catchy phrases or humour you don't want to forget, add them to your cue cards too.

Timing

Before closing this chapter, it is vital to talk about timing. If you've been asked to speak for ten minutes, take eight to ten. Not 15 and definitely not 20. A speaker who is oblivious to time, or worse, is aware but thinks he's so important he can just continue, is a chairperson's nightmare. It is always preferable to leave the audience wanting more of you than wishing you'd stop.

Pay attention to other people's presentation styles. Watch people in person and on television, consciously observing their techniques. Having read this chapter, you will find yourself noticing both their skills and their flaws. Have fun with it, making note of the characteristics you would like to adopt into your own public speaking method.

12

Beyond Firesides

'The Most Effective Method'

The Guardian feels that the most effective way for the Bahá'ís to teach the Faith is to make strong friends with their neighbours and associates. When the friends have confidence in the Bahá'ís and the Bahá'ís in their friends, they should give the Message and teach the Cause. Individual teaching of this type is more effective than any other type.

The principle of the fireside meeting, which was established in order to permit and encourage the individual to teach in his own home, has been proven the most effective instrument for spreading the Faith . . .

Written on behalf of Shoghi Effendi[55]

Success with Other Teaching Methods

In passages such as the one above the Guardian repeatedly tells us that fireside teaching is the most effective method. He does not, however, say that it is the *only* method. There are several other effective means Bahá'ís use to teach the Faith – advertising, holding public events, sponsoring conferences, dis-

tributing fliers, writing newspaper and magazine
articles, offering Unity Feasts, bringing guests to holy
day commemorations, establishing external affairs
connections, setting up display booths and so on. But
if fireside teaching is so effective, then why bother
with any other form of teaching? Why not just use
the most effective means? The Universal House of
Justice tells us that various methods must be used so
the Faith can be shared far and wide with all strata
of society:

> The same presentation of the teachings will not
> appeal to everybody; the method of expression and
> the approach must be varied in accordance with the
> outlook and interests of the hearer. An approach
> which is designed to appeal to everybody will usu-
> ally result in attracting the middle section, leaving
> both extremes untouched. No effort must be spared
> to ensure that the healing Word of God reaches the
> rich and the poor, the learned and the illiterate,
> the old and the young, the devout and the atheist,
> the dweller in the remote hills and islands, the
> inhabitant of the teeming cities, the suburban busi-
> nessman, the labourer in the slums, the nomadic
> tribesman, the farmer, the university student; all
> must be brought consciously within the teaching
> plans of the Bahá'í community.[56]

Mass teaching will reach the masses. Mass teaching
methods are commendable ways to alert the world
that Bahá'u'lláh's revelation is here. Bahá'ís can and
should pursue these teaching methods. The point I
am stressing, however, is that to apply these other

forms of teaching to the *exclusion* of firesides leaves a perilous gap in our teaching plans. Just as participation in prayer gatherings does not exempt us from saying our own daily obligatory prayers, taking part in teaching projects does not remove our duty to hold our own firesides at home.

I believe that firesides are the foundation upon which our other teaching rests. When new contacts show interest in the Faith because Bahá'ís are successfully teaching with other methods, firesides are necessary portals for the seekers to learn more. Bahá'ís cannot associate with new people only at proclamation events and keep their own homes out of bounds. If people are truly inspired by the Bahá'í Faith at a teaching event, they will want to know more. When these people are invited into Bahá'í homes they are able to inquire more deeply and have their questions answered. They also see the personal side of Bahá'í life. Everything the hosts do, from extending generous hospitality to respectfully listening to others, is being observed and no doubt admired.

A fireside is a small forum in which a Bahá'í practises teaching the Faith. Answering questions on a one-to-one basis with a friend is more comfortable for most people than public speaking. A Bahá'í gains teaching confidence in this relaxed setting. Through holding firesides, a Bahá'í develops teaching skills that will help him be even more effective when he participates in mass teaching events.

A letter written on behalf of the Guardian states:

In connection with the teaching work, the Guardian feels there is nothing more effective than the intimate fireside meeting in the home. He feels radio work, newspaper publicity, public meetings, etc. are of the utmost importance, but believes where people are confirmed is in the intimate fireside gatherings in the home. He feels the general basis of effective teaching is for the individual to make contacts, to develop these contacts into close friendship, so that the contacts have complete confidence in the individual, and then to gradually teach the individual the Cause. This will confirm the souls, and this work can certainly go on while publicity work is carried forward in the way of newspaper publicity, radio work and public meetings.[57]

I know a Bahá'í who detests street teaching. Proclaiming the Faith to strangers he meets at bus stops or in parks makes him extremely uncomfortable. 'Street teaching is for people who don't have any friends!' he jokes. He has plenty of personal friends whom he is teaching but he feels very awkward approaching strangers. He believes that a fireside at home is a more dignified teaching forum for him and he has become quite a successful fireside teacher.

But this Bahá'í also recognizes there is a legitimate place for proclamation techniques that are outside his comfort zone. Remaining obedient to the institutions of the Faith, this Bahá'í does support teaching projects initiated by his Local Spiritual Assembly, even when the events include teaching publicly. While he may not be able to be a front-line street teacher, he does support his community's teaching projects by assisting in deepenings for the teachers, chauffeuring them, printing brochures and so on. He has found resourceful ways to be part of projects by meeting some of the logistical needs while not teaching in ways he feels he cannot yet do.

Leadership from Assemblies

When I hear of a Bahá'í community planning a teaching project where one of the goals expressed is 'To have a fireside every day for a month' I wonder, 'If there are 19 Bahá'í households in that community, shouldn't there be at least 19 firesides happening anyway?' By educating the friends to hold monthly firesides, Assemblies avoid the awkward rush to have firesides during a teaching project.

If you are a member of a Local Spiritual Assembly, I urge you and your Assembly to educate the friends on the distinct nature and merit of firesides. Prioritize your community's development of firesides. This means more than just having a weekly 'community fireside' to which seekers can be referred. It means helping each and every Bahá'í understand and embrace his or her individual responsibility to hold firesides at home. An amazing transformation can take place when several households are holding regular firesides. Your community could rapidly expand.

Imagine for a moment each member of your community teaching and confirming one new person in the Cause each year. Would a doubling in your community's size each year feel like entry by troops to you? Indeed it would! Imagine how a doubling in size would change your community. Wonderful new challenges would occur, such as finding places to hold Feasts, organizing classes to deepen the new believers, having an increase in the local fund and so on. New Bahá'ís revitalize a community. Entry by troops is a reality waiting to happen. Anticipate the troops' arrival in your community!

Systematic Teaching

Indeed, much of the marked growth now being experienced by the Community of the Most Great Name may be attributed to efforts by an increasing number of National Spiritual Assemblies to devise and implement systematic teaching plans. Individual teaching infuses each community with a steady stream of new believers who, by virtue of their personal relationships with fellow-Bahá'ís, are easily integrated into the community. Systematic, collective efforts, on the other hand, open the doors to accelerated growth by focusing the collective energies of the friends on highly receptive populations. The high degree of unity invariably achieved through Group teaching, the intense use of prayer, and the sacrificial and disciplined life of the teachers, especially during campaigns, all contribute to attract and channel spiritual forces that indeed produce miracles.

The International Teaching Centre[58]

The various teaching methods – firesides, proclamation through media, display booths and so on – are not in competition with each other. They all form part of a community's systematic and comprehensive teaching plan. The International Teaching Centre also wrote:

> We feel confident that as the Counsellors and Auxiliary Board members, through individual contacts with the friends, through seminars, workshops and conferences, and especially in the context of institutes, help the friends gain insights into the spiritual nature of teaching, and increase their awareness of the complementarity of various approaches, the capacity of the Bahá'í community to grow will increase dramatically. The habit of contraposing one aspect of teaching against another — proclamation vs. teaching, expansion vs. consolidation, individual teaching vs. institutional plans, the fireside method vs. direct group teaching — will gradually give way to a mature outlook which comprehends the growth of the Bahá'í community in a more integral and harmonious way.[59]

My dear friend Dr Riḍván Moqbel relayed the following story which beautifully demonstrates the complementarity of various teaching methods:

> Several years ago I drove to the farm of a fellow Bahá'í, Neil Whatley. My wife and I were visiting in Saskatchewan and stayed two nights with Neil's family. When we arrived, Neil was still out in the field on his tractor. He waved as we drove up the driveway. We parked and got out of the car to wait

for him. The fresh air and quiet of the country were welcome changes to this city-dweller. Behind the house I could see Neil's father, a retired farmer, on his knees carefully weeding his small but immaculate vegetable garden. As I stood there leaning against the car, I marvelled at the juxtaposed beauty of the scene before me. Neil was riding his modern tractor, cultivating acres per day. And there was his father, patiently nurturing the vegetable garden, plant by plant. Neil's efforts would yield countless grains of wheat to feed hundreds of people. Meanwhile, the labour of love in the personal garden would produce enough vegetables for only an intimate group of family and friends.

To me this symbolized how we must teach the Bahá'í Faith. We must scatter the seeds of the Faith far and wide, reaching as many people as possible. We must also cultivate friendships and personally teach people in our homes. Certain teaching methods work best to reach the masses, while other methods are better for individual teaching. Both are necessary. Both yield fruit.

Individual Planning

Developing a comprehensive teaching plan is not only the job of Assemblies. The most successful teachers of the Cause have systematic personal teaching strategies. One's personal plan might answer the questions:

- How often will I have firesides and what kind shall they be?

- What creative ways can I use to proclaim the Faith?

- What contribution, no matter how large or small, can I make towards my Assembly's teaching plan?

- If my community does not yet have a clear teaching plan, how can I help develop one?

The role of the individual is of unique importance in the work of the Cause. It is the individual who manifests the vitality of faith upon which the success of the teaching work and the development of the community depend. Bahá'u'lláh's command to each believer to teach His Faith confers an inescapable responsibility which cannot be transferred to, or assumed by, any institution of the Cause. The individual alone can exercise those capacities which include the ability to take initiative, to seize opportunities, to form friendships, to interact personally with others, to build relationships, to win the cooperation of others in common service to the Faith and society, and to convert into action the decisions made by consultative bodies. It is the individual's duty to 'consider every avenue of approach which he might utilize in his personal attempts to capture the attention, maintain the interest, and deepen the faith, of those whom he seeks to bring into the fold of his Faith'.

The Universal House of Justice[60]

Conclusion

In its Riḍván message for the year 153 the Universal House of Justice wrote, 'The Four Year Plan aims at one major accomplishment: a significant advance in the process of entry by troops.'[61] To advance something means it is already in motion. Troops of people are hungering for Bahá'u'lláh's message. Let's not make the search any harder for them! Let's offer the Bahá'í Faith to them with 'the most effective method'.

> The Friends must arise with renewed spiritual enthusiasm, and confirm souls. The most important way to do this is the Fireside Gathering, where the souls can be closely associated with, and their detailed questions answered.
>
> *Written on behalf of Shoghi Effendi*[62]

Precious friend, I can urge you to share this magnificent Faith with all the people you possibly can but my encouragement remains powerless. It is *your* love for Bahá'u'lláh and your becoming totally immersed in His Will for you that will give you the ambition, conviction and ability to teach the Bahá'í Faith beyond your current achievements. It is the 'renewed spiritual enthusiasm' cited above that will excite you into action.

I hope this book has caused you to rethink your beliefs about firesides and has inspired you to have more of them. You have a distinct contribution to make towards winning the goals of the Cause. Turn the casual conversations in your home into part of a global furore of firesides.

As you reach the end of this book, I thank you for reading the thoughts of this student of the Cause. Before you move on to your next activity today, may I please make one final request of you? Could you set this book down now and pray? Submit yourself to the Will of Bahá'u'lláh, commit yourself to teaching His Cause and state your willingness to allow Him to show you the way.

Appendix

Bahá'í Writings for Further Enrichment

With so many encouraging quotations in the Bahá'í writings, it was not possible to include all the ones I would have liked to in the text of this book. This appendix contains a selection of writings on firesides and related teaching subjects from which I hope you draw further inspiration.

Firesides

The beloved Guardian attaches the utmost importance to . . . and urges the Friends in that city to arise as one soul in many bodies, filled with the enthusiasm of the Faith, and with complete dedication, consecration, and zeal, teach the Faith, individually, and collectively. Each one must establish as his goal for this year's work, the confirmation of at least one new Bahá'í. This can best be done by each individual determining to give the message to at least one person each day, and have a fireside gathering in his home each 19 days. In this way, each person will fulfil his divine responsibility, and win yet another victory for the Faith of God.

Written on behalf of Shoghi Effendi[63]

... I would like to comment that it has been found over the entire world that the most effective method of teaching the Faith is the fireside meeting in the home. Every Bahá'í as a part of his spiritual birthright, must teach, and the one avenue where he can do this most effectively is by inviting friends into his home once in 19 days, and gradually attracting them to the Cause. After the individuals have confidence in the pioneer, and the pioneer in the individuals, then they can be taught and confirmed in the Faith. This method is far more effective than advertising in newspapers, public lectures etc. The Guardian is encouraging the believers over the world, including those on the home fronts, to engage in this method of teaching.

Written on behalf of Shoghi Effendi[64]

. . . The fireside method of teaching seems to produce the greatest results; when each one invites friends into their homes once in 19 days, and introduces them to the Faith. Close association and loving service affects the hearts; and when the heart is affected, then the spirit can enter. It is the Holy Spirit that quickens, and the friends must become channels for its diffusion.

Written on behalf of Shoghi Effendi[65]

The Guardian was happy to learn of the teaching work in . . . This is a very important centre, and should have a strong community and Assembly. He hopes, therefore, that each of you will redouble your efforts – so the Faith may spread and grow. Each should invite Friends into his home for Fireside Gatherings, so that each will fulfil his responsibility to teach the Faith of God. If the proper spirit of dedication, consecration, and devoted action is taken, results will be achieved.

Written on behalf of Shoghi Effendi[66]

. . . One of the best ways to teach is what the Americans call a 'fireside', in other words a little group of your friends in your own home, to whom you can introduce a few believers whom you feel would be congenial and help confirm them. When you have made them true Bahá'ís, then take them to the community and let them be accepted. In this way they are protected from tests until their faith is really strong.

Written on behalf of Shoghi Effendi[67]

Qualities of the Teacher

As regards the teachers, they must completely divest themselves from the old garments and be invested with a new garment. According to the statement of Christ, they must attain to the station of rebirth – that is, whereas in the first instance they were born from the womb of the mother, this time they must be born from the womb of the world of nature. Just as they are now totally unaware of the experiences of the fetal world, they must also forget entirely the defects of the world of nature. They must be baptized with the water of life, the fire of the love of God and the breaths of the Holy Spirit; be satisfied with little food, but take a large portion from the heavenly table. They must disengage themselves from temptation and covetousness, and be filled with the spirit. Through the effect of their pure breath, they must change the stone into the brilliant ruby and the shell into pearl. Like unto the cloud of vernal shower, they must transform the black soil into the rosegarden and orchard. They must make the blind seeing, the deaf hearing, the extinguished one enkindled and set aglow, and the dead quickened.

Upon you be greetings and praise!

'Abdu'l-Bahá[68]

Teaching the faith is not conditioned by what occupation we have, or how great our knowledge is, but rather on how much we have studied the Teachings, to what degree we live the Bahá'í life, and how much we long to share this Message with others. When we have these characteristics, we are sure, if we search, to find receptive souls.

You should persevere and be confident that, with effort, success can be yours.

Written on behalf of Shoghi Effendi[69]

To be most effective, teaching needs more than proclamation. The message needs to be conveyed personally from one soul to another in a spirit of love. Shoghi Effendi talks about the 'art' of teaching. To excel in such an art requires courage, effort, constant application, the pain of uncertainty and an enormous willingness to take risks and suffer rebuffs. One needs wisdom and good judgement, and these the friends no doubt have in good measure. To them must be added audacity, joy, and confident reliance on the confirmations of the Holy Spirit. Ingenuity is also required, and perseverance. Although it may not be easy to meet people in order to teach them the Faith, let the friends never lose heart. There are ways if one seeks them with sufficient determination. Teaching the Faith comprises not merely offering a marvellous message, but conveying a feeling of enthusiasm and excitement at this message. After all, if we do not show people that we are enthusiastic about the Teachings of Bahá'u'lláh, how can we expect them to be enthusiastic?

The Universal House of Justice[70]

Victory of the Teaching Work

. . . Whosoever ariseth to aid our Cause God will render him victorious over ten times ten thousand souls, and, should he wax in his love for Me, him will We cause to triumph over all that is in heaven and all that is on earth.

Bahá'u'lláh[71]

Work! Work with all your strength, spread the Cause of the Kingdom among men; teach the self-sufficient to turn humbly towards God, the sinful to sin no more, and await with glad expectation the coming of the Kingdom.

Love and obey your Heavenly Father, and rest assured that Divine help is yours. Verily I say unto you that you shall indeed conquer the world!

Only have faith, patience and courage – this is but the beginning, but surely you will succeed, for God is with you!

'Abdu'l-Bahá[72]

The day is coming when all the religions of the world will unite, for in principle they are one already. There is no need for division, seeing that it is only the outward forms that separate them. Among the sons of men some souls are suffering through ignorance, let us hasten to teach them; others are like children needing care and education until they are grown, and some are sick – to these we must carry Divine healing.

'Abdu'l-Bahá[73]

Commanded to Teach

Say: To assist Me is to teach My Cause. This is a theme with which whole Tablets are laden. This is the changeless commandment of God, eternal in the past, eternal in the future.

Bahá'u'lláh[74]

In these days, the most important of all things is the guidance of the nations and peoples of the world. Teaching the Cause is of utmost importance for it is the head corner-stone of the foundation itself. This wronged servant has spent his days and nights in promoting the Cause and urging the peoples to service. He rested not a moment, till the fame of the Cause of God was noised abroad in the world and the celestial strains from the Abhá Kingdom roused the East and the West. The beloved of God must also follow the same example. This is the secret of faithfulness, this is the requirement of servitude to the Threshold of Bahá!

'Abdu'l-Bahá[75]

Bounties for the Teacher

Wert thou to open the heart of a single soul by helping him to embrace the Cause of Him Whom God shall make manifest, thine inmost being would be filled with the inspirations of that august Name. It devolveth upon you, therefore, to perform this task in the Days of Resurrection, inasmuch as most people are helpless, and wert thou to open their hearts and dispel their doubts, they would gain admittance into the Faith of God. Therefore, manifest thou this attribute to the utmost of thine ability in the days of Him Whom God shall make manifest. For indeed if thou dost open the heart of a person for His sake, better will it be for thee than every virtuous deed; since deeds are secondary to faith in Him and certitude in His Reality.

The Báb[76]

O thou dear handmaid of God! If only thou couldst know what a high station is destined for those souls who are severed from the world, are powerfully attracted to the Faith, and are teaching, under the sheltering shadow of Bahá'u'lláh! How thou wouldst rejoice, how thou wouldst, in exultation and rapture, spread thy wings and soar heavenward – for being a follower of such a way, and a traveller toward such a Kingdom.

'Abdu'l-Bahá[77]

In this day, the beloved of God must not hesitate or delay an instant in teaching the Cause of the Manifestation; and reconciling words of the religion of majestic oneness; because, verily, in this day, to the soul who is the cause of guidance to another soul the recompense of a martyr in the way of God will be assuredly recorded by the pen of the Cause for his deed. This is from the Bounty of God unto thee. Do according to what hast been commanded and do not be of those who tarry.

'Abdu'l-Bahá[78]

Divine Assistance

Purge thou thy heart that We may cause fountains of wisdom and utterance to gush out therefrom, thus enabling thee to raise thy voice among all mankind. Unloose thy tongue and proclaim the truth for the sake of the remembrance of thy merciful Lord. Be not afraid of anyone, place thy whole trust in God, the Almighty, the All-Knowing.

Bahá'u'lláh[79]

By the Lord of the Kingdom! If one arise to promote the Word of God with a pure heart, overflowing with the love of God and severed from the world, the Lord of Hosts will assist him with such a power as will penetrate the core of the existent beings.

'Abdu'l-Bahá[80]

How to Speak

Every word is endowed with a spirit, therefore the speaker or expounder should carefully deliver his words at the appropriate time and place, for the impression which each word maketh is clearly evident and perceptible. The Great Being saith: One word may be likened unto fire, another unto light, and the influence which both exert is manifest in the world. Therefore an enlightened man of wisdom should primarily speak with words as mild as milk, that the children of men may be nurtured and edified thereby and may attain the ultimate goal of human existence which is the station of true understanding and nobility.

Bahá'u'lláh[81]

Proclaim the Cause of thy Lord unto all who are in the heavens and on the earth. Should any man respond to thy call, lay bare before him the pearls of the wisdom of the Lord, thy God, which His Spirit hath sent down unto thee, and be thou of them that truly believe. And should any one reject thine offer, turn thou away from him, and put thy trust and confidence in the Lord, thy God, the Lord of all worlds.

Bahá'u'lláh[82]

If their task is to be confined to good conduct and advice, nothing will be accomplished. They must speak out, expound the proofs, set forth clear arguments, draw irrefutable conclusions establishing the truth of the manifestation of the Sun of Reality.

'Abdu'l-Bahá[83]

Exerting Influence

It behoveth the people of Bahá to render the Lord victorious through the power of their utterance and to admonish the people by their goodly deeds and character, inasmuch as deeds exert greater influence than words.

Bahá'u'lláh[84]

O My Name! Utterance must needs possess penetrating power. For if bereft of this quality it would fail to exert influence. And this penetrating influence dependeth on the spirit being pure and the heart stainless. Likewise it needeth moderation, without which the hearer would be unable to bear it, rather he would manifest opposition from the very outset. And moderation will be obtained by blending utterance with the tokens of divine wisdom which are recorded in the sacred Books and Tablets. Thus when the essence of one's utterance is endowed with these two requisites it will prove highly effective and will be the prime factor in transforming the souls of men. This is the station of supreme victory and celestial dominion. Whoso attaineth thereto is invested with the power to teach the Cause of God and to prevail over the hearts and minds of men.

Bahá'u'lláh[85]

Human utterance is an essence which aspireth to exert its influence and needeth moderation. As to its influence, this is conditional upon refinement which in turn is dependent upon hearts which are detached and pure. As to its moderation, this hath to be combined with tact and wisdom as prescribed in the Holy Scriptures and Tablets.

Bahá'u'lláh[86]

The Word of God is the king of words and its pervasive influence is incalculable. It hath ever dominated and will continue to dominate the realm of being. The Great Being saith: The Word is the master key for the whole world, inasmuch as through its potency the doors of the hearts of men, which in reality are the doors of heaven, are unlocked . . . It is an ocean inexhaustible in riches, comprehending all things. Every thing which can be perceived is but an emanation therefrom.

Bahá'u'lláh[87]

The teacher, when teaching, must be himself fully enkindled, so that his utterance, like unto a flame of fire, may exert influence and consume the veil of self and passion. He must also be utterly humble and lowly so that others may be edified, and be totally self-effaced and evanescent so that he may teach with the melody of the Concourse on high – otherwise his teaching will have no effect.

'Abdu'l-Bahá[88]

Consolidation

Teaching the Faith embraces many diverse activities, all of which are vital to success, and each of which reinforce the other. Time and again the beloved Guardian emphasized that expansion and consolidation are twin and inseparable aspects to teaching that must proceed simultaneously yet one still hears believers discussing the virtues of one as against the other. The purpose of teaching is not complete when a person declares that he has accepted Bahá'u'lláh as the Manifestation of God for this age; the purpose of teaching is to attract human beings to the Divine Message and so imbue them with its spirit that they will dedicate themselves to its service, and this world will become another world and its people another people. Viewed in this light a declaration of Faith is merely a milestone along the way – albeit a very important one. Teaching may also be likened to kindling a fire, the fire of faith, in the hearts of men. If a fire burns only so long as the match is held to it, it cannot truly be said to have been kindled; to be kindled it must continue to burn of its own accord. Thereafter more fuel can be added and the flame can be fanned, but even if left alone for a period, a truly kindled fire will not be extinguished by the first breath of wind.

The Universal House of Justice[89]

Bibliography

'Abdu'l-Bahá. *Selections from the Writings of 'Abdu'l-Bahá.* Haifa: Bahá'í World Centre, 1978.

— *Tablets of the Divine Plan.* Wilmette, Ill.: Bahá'í Publishing Trust, 1993.

— *The Will and Testament of 'Abdu'l-Bahá.* Wilmette, Ill.: Bahá'í Publishing Trust, 1971.

The Báb. *Selections from the Writings of the Báb.* Haifa: Bahá'í World Centre, 1976.

Bahá'í World, The. vols. 1–12, 1925–54. rpt. Wilmette, Ill.: Bahá'í Publishing Trust, 1980.

Bahá'u'lláh. *Gleanings from the Writings of Bahá'u'lláh.* Wilmette, Ill.: Bahá'í Publishing Trust, 1983.

— *The Kitáb-i-Aqdas.* Haifa: Bahá'í World Centre, 1992.

— *Tablets of Bahá'u'lláh revealed after the Kitáb-i-Aqdas.* Haifa: Bahá'í World Centre, 1978.

Compilation of Compilations, The. Prepared by the Universal House of Justice 1963–1990. 2 vols. [Sydney]: Bahá'í Publications Australia, 1991.

The Greatest Gift. Compiled by the National Teaching Committee of the National Spiritual Assembly of the Bahá'ís of Canada. Toronto, 1970.

Keenness of Vision. Reference Materials for Auxiliary Board Members and Assistants, prepared by the Continental Board of Counsellors in Europe. 2nd edn., 1994.

Lights of Guidance: A Bahá'í Reference File. Compiled by Helen Hornby. New Delhi: Bahá'í Publishing Trust, 2nd edn. 1988.

Maxwell, May. *An Early Pilgrimage*. Oxford: George Ronald, 1976.

Rabbani, Rúḥíyyih. *A Manual for Pioneers*. New Delhi: Bahá'í Publishing Trust, 1974.

Shoghi Effendi. *The Advent of Divine Justice*. Wilmette, Ill.: Bahá'í Publishing Trust, 1990.

— *Dawn of a New Day: Messages to India 1923–1957*. New Delhi: Bahá'í Publishing Trust, 1970.

— *Messages to the Bahá'í World*. Wilmette, Ill.: Bahá'í Publishing Trust, 1971.

The Universal House of Justice. *The Four Year Plan*. Riviera Beach, Florida: Palabra Publications, 1996.

— *Wellspring of Guidance*. Wilmette, Ill.: Bahá'í Publishing Trust, 1976.

References and Notes

1. Bahá'u'lláh, *Gleanings*, p. 335.
2. ibid. p. 278.
3. Shoghi Effendi, *Advent of Divine Justice*, p. 45.
4. Bahá'u'lláh, *Gleanings*, p. 335.
5. From a letter written on behalf of Shoghi Effendi to a Local Spiritual Assembly and an individual believer, 11 December 1952, in *Compilation*, vol. 2, p. 317.
6. The Universal House of Justice, Riḍván Message 1987.
7. From a letter of the Universal House of Justice to a National Spiritual Assembly in Europe, 12 September 1991.
8. Bahá'u'lláh, *Gleanings*, p. 330.
9. 'Abdu'l-Bahá, *Selections*, p. 265.
10. Bahá'u'lláh, *Gleanings*, p. 314.
11. ibid. p. 278.
12. ibid. p. 280.
13. Bahá'u'lláh, *Kitáb-i-Aqdas*, para. 53.
14. Bahá'u'lláh, *Gleanings*, pp. 196–7.
15. ibid. p. 314.
16. The Báb, *Selections*, p. 77.
17. From a letter written on behalf of Shoghi Effendi to an individual believer, in *Bahá'í World*, vol. 5, p. 126.
18. From a letter written on behalf of Shoghi Effendi to the National Spiritual Assembly of the United States, 21 September 1957, in *Compilation*, vol. 2, p. 27.

19. From a letter written on behalf of Shoghi Effendi to an individual believer, 20 October 1956, in ibid. p. 323.
20. From a letter written on behalf of Shoghi Effendi to an individual believer, 6 March 1957, in *Lights of Guidance*, p. 248.
21. From a letter written on behalf of Shoghi Effendi to an individual believer, 20 October 1956, in *Compilation*, vol. 2, p. 323.
22. From a letter written on behalf of Shoghi Effendi to a National Spiritual Assembly, 4 July 1957, cited in a letter from the Research Department at the Bahá'í World Centre to the author, 22 April 1998.
23. Attributed to 'Abdu'l-Bahá, cited in Rabbani, *A Manual for Pioneers*, p. 4.
24. Bahá'u'lláh, *Tablets*, p. 200.
25. 'Abdu'l-Bahá, quoted in Maxwell, *An Early Pilgrimage*, p. 40.
26. Bahá'u'lláh, *Gleanings*, p. 141.
27. 'Abdu'l-Bahá, *Selections*, p. 30.
28. Bahá'u'lláh, *Kitáb-i-Aqdas*, para. 52.
29. The Universal House of Justice, in ibid. note 80.
30. 'Abdu'l-Bahá, *Selections*, p. 80.
31. Shoghi Effendi, *Dawn of a New Day*, p. 86.
32. From a letter written on behalf of Shoghi Effendi to an individual believer, 14 March 1955, in *Lights of Guidance*, p. 478.
33. From a letter of the Universal House of Justice to a National Spiritual Assembly, 7 October 1973, in *Lights of Guidance*, p. 108.
34. From a letter written on behalf of the Universal House of Justice to a National Spiritual Assembly, 13 March 1969, in ibid. p. 109.
35. 'Abdu'l-Bahá, in *Compilation*, vol. 2, pp. 246–7.

36.   Shoghi Effendi, *Advent of Divine Justice*, p. 30.
37.   The Báb, *Selections*, p. 217.
38.   From a letter written on behalf of Shoghi Effendi to an individual believer, 21 May 1954, in *Lights of Guidance*, p. 364.
39.   From a letter of the Universal House of Justice to an individual believer, 12 January 1973, in ibid. p. 365.
40.   From a letter written on behalf of the Universal House of Justice to an individual believer, 9 January 1977, in ibid. p. 366.
41.   From letter written on behalf of Shoghi Effendi to the National Assembly of Germany and Austria, 28 May 1954, in ibid. p. 241.
42.   From a letter written on behalf of the Universal House of Justice to the National Spiritual Assembly of Belgium, 4 November 1967, in *Compilation*, vol. 1, p. 445.
43.   From a letter written on behalf of Shoghi Effendi to two believers, 21 September 1946, in ibid. p. 443.
44.   From a letter written on behalf of the Universal House of Justice to an individual believer, 12 August 1981, in ibid. p. 445.
45.   'Abdu'l-Bahá, *Selections*, p. 30.
46.   Rúḥíyyih Rabbani, *Manual for Pioneers*, p.42.
47.   Bahá'u'lláh, *Gleanings*, p. 176.
48.   From a letter written on behalf of Shoghi Effendi to an individual believer, 24 February 1950. Cited in a letter from the Research Department at the Bahá'í World Centre to the author, 22 April 1998.
49.   'The Bahá'ís are free to greet each other with Alláh-u-Abhá when they meet, if they want to, but they should avoid anything which to outsiders, in a western country, might seem like some strange oriental password. We must be very firm on princi-

ples and laws, but very normal and natural in our ways, so as to attract strangers!' From a letter written on behalf of Shoghi Effendi to an individual believer, 17 July 1951, in *Lights of Guidance*, p. 266.

50. National Teaching Committee of Canada, *The Greatest Gift*, p. 11.
51. Bahá'u'lláh, *Kitáb-i-Aqdas*, para. 38.
52. The Universal House of Justice, *Wellspring of Guidance*, p. 32.
53. Bahá'u'lláh, *Tablets*, pp. 236–7.
54. Bahá'u'lláh, *Gleanings*, pp. 105–6.
55. From a letter written on behalf of Shoghi Effendi to an individual believer, 27 December 1954, in *Compilation*, vol. 2, p. 319.
56. Letter of the Universal House of Justice, 31 October 1967, in The Universal House of Justice, *Wellspring of Guidance*, p. 124.
57. From a letter written on behalf of Shoghi Effendi to an individual believer, 27 April 1954. Cited in a letter from the Research Department at the Bahá'í World Centre to the author, 22 April 1998.
58. From a letter of the International Teaching Centre to all Counsellors, 21 October 1990, in *Keenness of Vision*, p. 39.
59. ibid. p. 40.
60. Message of the Universal House of Justice to the Bahá'ís of the World, Riḍván 153, in *The Four Year Plan*, para. 3.20.
61. ibid. para. 3.17.
62. From a letter written on behalf of Shoghi Effendi to an individual believer, 20 October 1956. Cited in a letter from the Research Department at the Bahá'í World Centre to the author, 22 April 1998.

63.   From a letter written on behalf of Shoghi Effendi to an individual believer, 4 July 1954. Cited in a letter from the Research Department at the Bahá'í World Centre to the author, 22 April 1998.

64.   From a letter written on behalf of Shoghi Effendi to the Bahá'í Group of Key West, Florida, 31 March 1955, in *Lights of Guidance*, p. 247.

65.   From a letter written on behalf of Shoghi Effendi to an individual believer, 27 January 1957, in ibid. p. 248.

66.   From a letter written on behalf of Shoghi Effendi to a couple, 9 April 1957. Cited in a letter from the Research Department at the Bahá'í World Centre to the author, 22 April 1998.

67.   From a letter written on behalf of Shoghi Effendi to an individual believer, 18 March 1950, in *Lights of Guidance*, p. 248.

68.   'Abdu'l-Bahá, *Tablets of the Divine Plan*, p. 96.

69.   From a letter written on behalf of Shoghi Effendi to an American believer, 1957, in *Lights of Guidance*, p. 585.

70.   From a letter of the Universal House of Justice to a National Spiritual Assembly in Europe, 12 September 1991.

71.   Bahá'u'lláh, quoted in Shoghi Effendi, *Messages to the Bahá'í World*, p. 101.

72.   'Abdu'l-Bahá, *Paris Talks*, p. 101.

73.   ibid. p. 121.

74.   Bahá'u'lláh, *Tablets*, p. 196.

75.   'Abdu'l-Bahá, *Will and Testament*, p. 10.

76.   The Báb, *Selections*, p. 133.

77.   'Abdu'l-Bahá, *Selections*, p. 100.

78.   'Abdu'l-Bahá, in *Lights of Guidance*, p. 585.

79.   Bahá'u'lláh, *Tablets*, pp. 189–90.

80. 'Abdu'l-Bahá, in *Compilation*, vol. 2, p. 211.
81. Bahá'u'lláh, *Tablets*, pp. 172–3.
82. 'Abdu'l-Bahá, *Selections*, p. 268.
83. Bahá'u'lláh, *Gleanings*, p. 280.
84. Bahá'u'lláh, *Tablets*, p. 57.
85. ibid. pp. 198–9.
86. ibid. p. 143.
87. ibid. p. 173.
88. 'Abdu'l-Bahá, *Selections*, p. 270.
89. From a letter of the Universal House of Justice to all National Spiritual Assemblies, 25 May 1975, in *Lights of Guidance*, pp. 594–5.